Higher Grad Computing Studies Revision Notes

Arlen Pardoe
Principal Teacher of Computing Studies
Madras College, St. Andrews

and

Kevin Thompson
Principal Teacher of Computing Studies
Queen Anne High School, Dunfermline

Published by Leckie & Leckie
8 Whitehill Terrace
St. Andrews KY16 8RN
Tel. 01334 - 475656
Fax. 01334 - 477392

Edited by Neil Kennedy

Thanks also to Bruce Ryan, Hamish Sanderson and Nolan Cocker

ISBN 1-898890-50-1

A CIP Catalogue record for this book is available from the British Library.

Leckie & Leckie

Contents

1. Introduction

1. Higher Grade Computing Studies

Your Higher Grade course provides you with the computing skills, knowledge and competence to use new technologies for personal and work-related purposes. The emphasis is on understanding and application of general concepts and competences, rather than concentrating on specific characteristics of existing systems. A range of different types of system and users exists and the area of computing is one where change is rapid.

Within this context it is still important to be competent at using computers and you will probably only have the opportunity to study one type of system, using one example each of a general purpose package and a programming language. You must be aware that this is a limited view of a complex subject.

2. Preparation for the examination

There is no substitute for proper preparation for examinations. You have made a good start by obtaining these Revision Notes! However, on their own they will not guarantee success.

Firstly, you must use them in conjunction with the course materials provided by your teacher. These Notes should direct your attention to the main topics which you can then revise more fully from the school materials.

Secondly, do not expect to revise in a short period of time. Give yourself the opportunity to read and reread all your course notes. Effective planning of the topics and their revision can be helped by drawing up a schedule of revision. Force yourself to keep to it!

3. Course themes

A number of themes are identified with applications and correspond with all the major topics of your course.

Two broad themes are identified:

- Stimulus to development - what are the factors which led to the development of the particular application?
- Implications - the wider social, economic and technical consequences of the use of the application.

Four further themes are identified by considering the factors in the design of computer systems which are concerned with how easily and effectively the user communicates with the computer. These can be used as a basis of comparing a range of computer uses:

- Integration - hardware and software working together, transferring data between different systems and application packages.
- Levels of software - choosing the best level for the user communicating with the computer for a specific purpose.
- Objects and operations - the facilities available to the user at a particular level of software.
- Human computer interface - the ease of use of a system in terms of facilities offered and documentation.

The overall purpose of these six themes is to allow a comprehensive comparison of existing and new applications.

4. What these Notes cover

These Revision Notes cover the core topics of the Higher Grade course. They do not cover the optional case studies. Only the general features of programming languages, general purpose packages and systems are covered, in line with the general philosophy of the course itself.

2. General Purpose Packages

Introduction

1. Problem-solving Tools
General Purpose Packages (GPPs) were developed to solve common computing problems. A GPP is a program (or programs), together with documentation, which allows the user to solve a range of similar problems.

2. Why GPPs were developed
Early computers used simple input and output devices, were slow and had little memory. They were very expensive, difficult to program and were used by very few people. As technology advanced, more people came to use computers and programming languages were developed. Some large businesses owned computers and programs were specially written for them. By the advent of personal computers in the late 1970s and early 1980s, computers were common in businesses and were used by people who were not experts. It was not feasible for each individual inexpert user to have programs written for them. This led to the development of GPPs.

3. The main GPPs

Four major GPPs are studied:	typical examples:
• Word Processing	Microsoft Word WordPerfect
• Spreadsheets	Microsoft Excel Lotus 1, 2, 3
• Databases	Filemaker Pro dBase
• Graphic packages	Adobe Photoshop Corel Draw

4. Other Applications
A variety of other types of applications can be identified and may be regarded as GPPs in their own right. These include communications packages, presentation packages and desktop publishing packages.

5. Objects and Operations
Identification of the objects to be manipulated and the operations to be carried out on them is an aid in deciding which GPP is best suited for a particular problem.

- Objects are the data objects to be manipulated. These may be small, such as a single character, a word or a pixel; they may be large, such as a paragraph or a complete document.
- Operations are the processes carried out on objects. For example, cutting, deleting, sorting or resizing.

6. The analytical approach
looks for the best solution to a problem by analysing its requirements. In particular, the **objects** required by the problem and the **operations** carried out on those objects will determine the best solution.
Once the objects and operations have been identified then a language must be available in which the objects and operations can be used. It is best if these are already present, though a language which allows you to define new operations has an advantage over one that is less flexible and does not allow such definitions to take place.

quick check

General Purpose Package (GPP). Reasons for development of GPPs. Word-processor, spreadsheet, database, graphics package. Other applications. Objects and operations. Analytical approach to solving problems.

7. Syntax and Semantics

A more effective comparison of languages can be made by separately identifying these processes.

- **Syntax** is the set of rules governing the way in which elements of the language are put together to make a meaningful statement. Breaking the rules results in an illegal statement (one which is ambiguous or cannot be understood).
- **Semantics** is concerned with the meaning of language statements which obey the rules of the language - what the effect is when the instruction is carried out.

Examples of different syntax and semantics are given later in the area of study for languages.

8. Features of the main GPPs

- Word-processing packages manipulate text. A wide range of tools is provided for this purpose. Although other GPPs also use text, they have a much more limited choice of tools.

- Spreadsheet packages use a cell layout and allow manipulation of text and numeric data. A wide range of functions is provided for mathematical operations on numbers. These often use cell references for calculations.

- Database packages organise text and numeric data and allow retrieval of information in a wide variety of forms and presentations. A variety of search options gives considerable flexibility. Large amounts of data can be organised very quickly.

- Graphic packages are designed for the manipulation of graphical data, charts, diagrams and pictures. The two main graphical formats, bit-mapped and object-oriented, are usually addressed by different packages.

9. Implications of GPPs

Complex issues arise when the subject of the widespread use of GPPs is investigated. The use of the computer is taken away from the few experts and given to the more general population. The effect on employment is considerable. Traditional jobs disappear and new ones appear (typesetting -v- word-processing staff). It is similar for manufacturers (typewriter -v- printer manufacturers). Offices in particular have been affected, with an impact especially on the employment of traditionally female and part-time staff. Businesses which do not keep up with these changes disappear. For example, travel agents expect immediate access to databases to book holidays; as soon as the booking is made those places are removed from sale. Any travel agent not using this technology will not survive. The filing power of databases and the word-processing power of word-processors give the company using them a greater office productivity than those without, so increasing efficiency and reducing costs. Other issues appear which are concerned with the widespread availability of information coupled with easy access. The security of this data, and the types of information which people have access to, is controversial. The Data Protection Act attempts to address some of these concerns. New technological advances, such as multimedia and the Internet, increase both the appeal and the availability of information in textual and graphical form. Future developments in communications technology will make this even more accessible.

10. Areas of study

When studying GPPs, four areas are identified:

- Matching the package to the application
- Languages used in GPPs
- Human Computer Interface
- Package integration

quick check

Syntax, semantics. Features of main GPPs. Implications of GPPs. Areas of study.

Matching the package to the application

1. What package to use?

Each class of GPP has data objects which are typical to that package. Operations that can be carried out on the objects can be identified.
Some objects and their associated operations are very common and are found in most or all GPPs. These are summarised on page 7. Others are more relevant to individual packages and therefore are important in deciding what package to use in solving a particular problem.
Considering the objects and operations for a particular problem can help decide on the most suitable package to use.

- Objects associated with Word-processing
  - characters, words, sentences, paragraphs, document, section, footnote
  - header, footer, line, page
  - continuous segment
- Word-processing operations
  - create, insert, select, delete, search, format
  - set sizes, annotate
  - change style, cut, paste

- Objects associated with Databases
  file, record, field
  report (subset)
- Database operations
  search, sort, update, replicate, compute field, format

- Objects associated with Spreadsheets
  cell containing entered text (constant text)
  cell containing entered numbers (constant value)
  cell containing calculated data (formula or function)
- Spreadsheet operations
  evaluate (calculate), sort, replicate

- Objects associated with Graphics
  line, arc, area, shape, diagram, picture
- Graphic operations
  draw, scale, translate, rotate

2. Overlap between packages

Modern GPPs are very different to those which were originally developed to solve common problems. There is considerable overlap and even 'simple' packages offer facilities associated with other classes of GPP. This overlap allows users to carry out operations without having to move between packages. However, they are more complex and require more memory.
As an example, the ability to draw simple shapes such as lines and rectangles is one associated with graphics packages, but is now found in almost every other class of GPP, and certainly in a word-processor, database or spreadsheet written for a modern system.

A second example of overlap is the ability of a spreadsheet package to draw complex graphs and charts from spreadsheet data. Modern spreadsheets allow a wide variety such as pie charts, scatter charts, bar charts, together with substantial control over axes and labels.
As a third example, most modern spreadsheets allow parts of the spreadsheet to be declared as a database and typical database operations can be carried out, such as selecting a subset according to specifications provided, or complex searches.

quick check

Matching the package to the application, objects and operations associated with the main GPPs.
Overlap between packages.

3. Common operations usually offered by most GPPs

- Working with text - Most GPPs have tools for using text. They usually allow the size, font (or typeface) and style to be changed; text can be selected, cut, copied and pasted. However, word-processing operations such as spellchecking, applying styles or adding footnotes will not generally be provided.

- Editing operations - are used in all GPPs to allow objects to be entered, altered and deleted. This may be text in a word-processor, field contents in a database, cell contents in a spreadsheet or the size of a rectangle in a graphics package.

- Selection of objects - In order to carry out operations on objects, the GPP must allow them to be selected. This may involve the insertion of special marking characters, or the use of cursor keys or a mouse to highlight the objects.

- Calculation of values - for example, page numbers or dates in a word-processing package; scaling objects in a graphics package; adding together contents of fields in a database; or using formulas or functions in a cell of a spreadsheet.

- Handling documents - covers operations dealing with the layout of a document, such as the size and orientation of a page, the margins set for the page and header and footer information.

- Pattern matching (searching) - in word-processed documents looks for words, particularly in search and replace or using a partial match; in databases selects a subset, perhaps using several search criteria; in spreadsheets uses lookup tables, where a value is returned based on the data provided. When specifying file and directory names the operating system may allow pattern matching (for example, the use of * or ? in path names).

- Use of backing storage - Since it is always necessary to save application files containing data on backing storage, and to be able to load them back at a later time, the minimum requirement is to save and load documents. Other facilities may also be available, such as duplicating, saving under a different name or deleting files when using the application.

4. Database or spreadsheet?

It sometimes happens that a problem can be solved using more than one package. Sometimes this is resolved if only one package is available. For example, you could use a spreadsheet as a word-processor if that was the only package available and the task was not too complex. However, it would usually be better to use a word-processor. Some tasks in particular seem to be able to be solved by either a database or a spreadsheet. There are advantages to each type of package which may make it the preferred choice.

- Databases offer:
  - better searching and sorting facilities, allowing complex criteria to be set up
  - considerable control over the way in which data is presented
  - calculations usually within one record; calculations between records can usually only be done within one field.
- Spreadsheets offer:
  - more complex functions such as lookup tables, often used for accounting purposes
  - calculations based on any cells in the spreadsheet
  - graph plotting facilities
  - Modern spreadsheets allow a group of cells to be used as databases.

quick check

Common GPP operations - using text, editing, selection, calculation, document handling, searching, using backing storage. Database -v- spreadsheet.

Languages

1. Languages

A language is required to communicate with a computer. This is obvious if you are using a high or low level language to program the computer, where you are using some form of text. However, language is concerned with communication and humans can communicate without using words, for example by using symbols or sign language. In communicating with the computer, other forms of language exist, each with their own syntax and semantics.

It is common for different ways of communication to exist between the user and the computer where the same instructions are given using very different syntax and perhaps using different language. It is also possible to compare two languages and find that the same syntax has entirely different meanings.

2. Various types of syntax

The syntax rules will vary according to the way in which the statement or command is made. The requirements of a text environment may seem different to those of a WIMP environment but the basic principles are the same.

For example, you may wish to underline a section of text in a printed document. In one package this may require the insertion of special instructions telling the printer to start or stop underlining the characters:

```
This is an example of OC 27,69 text
which is underlined OC 27,70
```

Here, the word does not appear on screen underlined as it would appear in the printed document. This is a more primitive application than one which shows exactly what will be printed on screen (WYSIWYG). However, some current applications use a similar approach, for example Postscript language (a page description language for printers) and HTML (used to create WWW pages on the Internet).

The same effect may be accomplished by a different syntax in modern applications. The words to be underlined are selected (using mouse or cursor keys) and the underline option is selected. This may be carried out by a menu option on the screen, or by keyboard command.

3. Languages in one package

It is possible that one package can carry out the same operation using a different language. In the last example, the underline operation was specified by a menu choice.

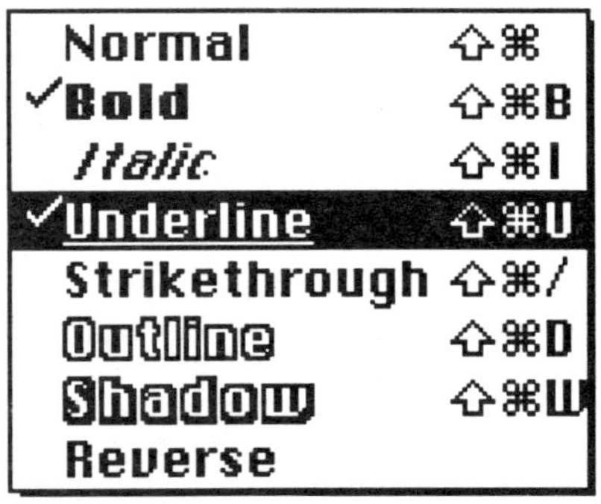

The menu window also shows a second way of making this choice, with a combination of keys (in this example, shift - command - U). Other systems may also use special keys on the keyboard called function keys. Thus, underlining selected words could be carried out by using the mouse (or cursor keys) to select from a menu, or by a combination of keys on the keyboard. The reason for having two levels of language is to provide a system that is:

- easy for the inexperienced user to use (menu choice, where all the possible operations are presented).
- suited to the experienced user (keyboard action, no need to take hand from keyboard to use mouse but need to know the key combination).

quick check

Languages. Different types of syntax. Different languages in the same package.

4. Various types of semantics
It is possible for the same syntax to have different semantics. This is not reasonable in the same package, operating on similar objects. However, it commonly exists when moving from one package to another. This can cause much confusion with users.

An example within the same package is dragging an object in a WIMP system to the wastebasket. If the object is the icon for a file, it may mean 'delete the file'. If the object is the icon for a floppy disc, it may mean 'eject the floppy disc'.

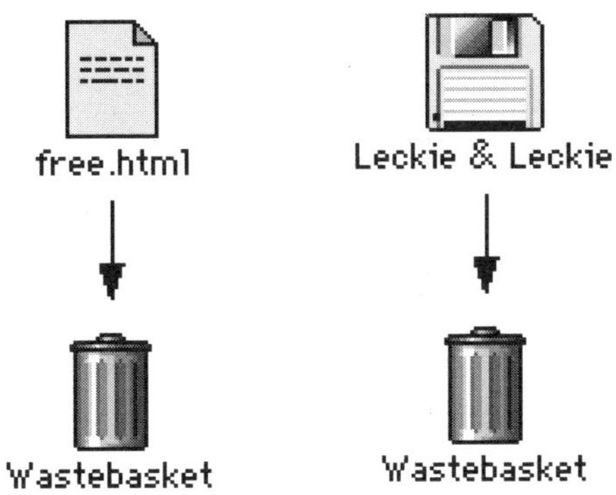

delete the document — eject the disc

An example between packages is using the key combination, command - B. In one package this may mean 'make the text selected or following bold'; in another package it may mean 'clear the selected cells'.

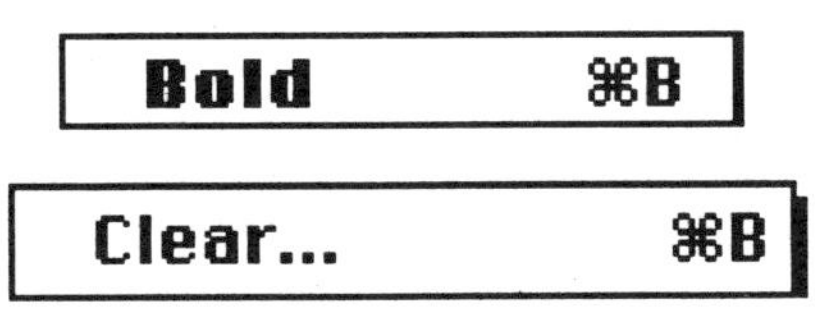

5. Fourth Generation Languages
are a set of languages which have been developed to solve problems in a variety of application areas, especially databases. They use a language at a higher level than conventional programming languages to generate code.

The advantage of such a system is that it allows expert users to tailor an application to their exact needs. This is a much more efficient process than trying to write an application from scratch.

6. Macros
provide a means of giving a single command to carry out a series of operations.
A macro may be set up by recording the actual commands as they are carried out. They can then be replayed when required. Alternatively, a special macro language might be used to give instructions similar to high level languages.
The execution of a macro might be started in a variety of ways:

- using a function key or combination of keys
- selecting from a menu
- executing a batch file.

Macros are used either to carry out a frequently used series of commands, or to simplify an otherwise complex task. A simple example in the first category is a macro to place your name and address at the start of a letter; for the complex task it could involve sorting invoices into a given order and selecting only those due to a given supplier for printing.

quick check

Types of semantics. Fourth generation languages. Macros.

Human Computer Interface (HCI)

1. Human Computer Interface

This describes the way in which the computer and the human user interact. It includes a variety of related factors such as:

- styles of HCI
- methods of giving commands
- peripherals used
- ergonomics

The HCI is studied to improve the ease with which humans can interact with the computer.

2. Styles of HCI

The HCI has historically gone through a variety of phases, mainly associated with technological advances:

- the earliest interface consisted of banks of switches for input and rows of lights for output. This was slow and complex to use.
- later HCIs used punched cards and paper tape for input and teletypes (a kind of electric typewriter) for output.
- more recent HCIs commonly use mouse or keyboard input and output to monitor.

A number of styles of interaction can be identified, for example:

- for <u>text-only displays</u>.
- for <u>low to medium resolution</u> displays, using simple graphics and colour and mainly the cursor keys for activities.
- for <u>high-resolution</u> graphics displays using precise input with such devices as a mouse, trackerball, graphic tablet, joystick or touch screen for activities.

3. Text-only displays

- menu selection
- form filling
- split screen
- help facilities
- on-line documentation
- error messages

3. Text-only displays (cont.)

Menu selection

```
LeckieSoft WordPro 1.0

    1. Load text
    2. Save text
    3. Print text
    4. Check spelling
    5. Search & replace
    6. Go to edit screen

    Select (1-6)?▒
```

Form filling

```
Leckiesoft QuickAccount 2.0

Account no - 412▒....
Name       - ..............
Address    - ..............
             ..............
             ..............

Dated - ../../..  Our ref - ....
```

Split screen

```
LeckieSoft SheetPro 1.2
53 16 ▒. . . . . . . . . . . . .
 . . . . . . . . . . . . . . . .
 . . . . . . . . . . . . . . . .
 . . . . . . . . . . . . . . . .
 . . . . . . . . . . . . . . . .
--------------------------------
F1 Formula       F4 Add column
F2 Replicate     F5 Load file
F3 Add row       F6 Save file
```

Help facilities

```
>*HELP

DFS 1.20
  DFS
  UTILS
NFS 3.60
OS 1.20

>▒
```

On-line documentation

```
      Toolkit Help Menu

   C to copy
   M to move
   F to find
   D to delete
   P to print

   Press ESC to return
   to main menu
```

Error messages

```
Disk fault 18 at 00/00

>▒
```

quick check

Human Computer Interface. Styles of HCI. Text-only displays.

4. **Low to medium resolution**

- teletext and videotext displays

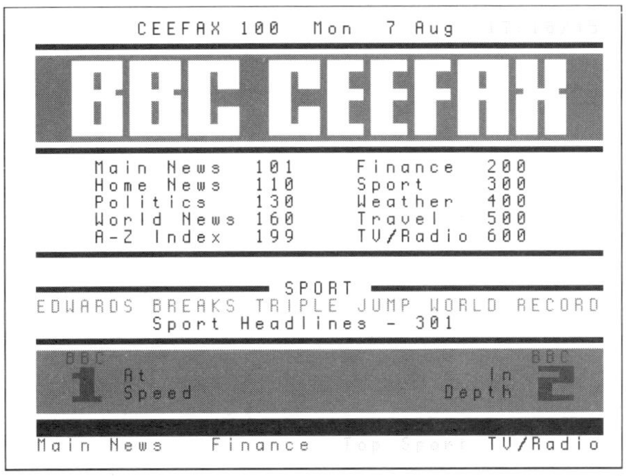

This type of display is characterised by information presented as text of a fixed size together with simple graphic characters. To present larger text, or simple graphics, the graphic characters are joined together on screen. The result is an angular object with the 'building blocks' being very obvious.

5. **High resolution**

- icon based interfaces (WIMP systems)
  - windows
    This example shows three windows laid one on top of another. The upper window, Accessories, is the one in current use; below that is the window Main and below that the window Program Manager.

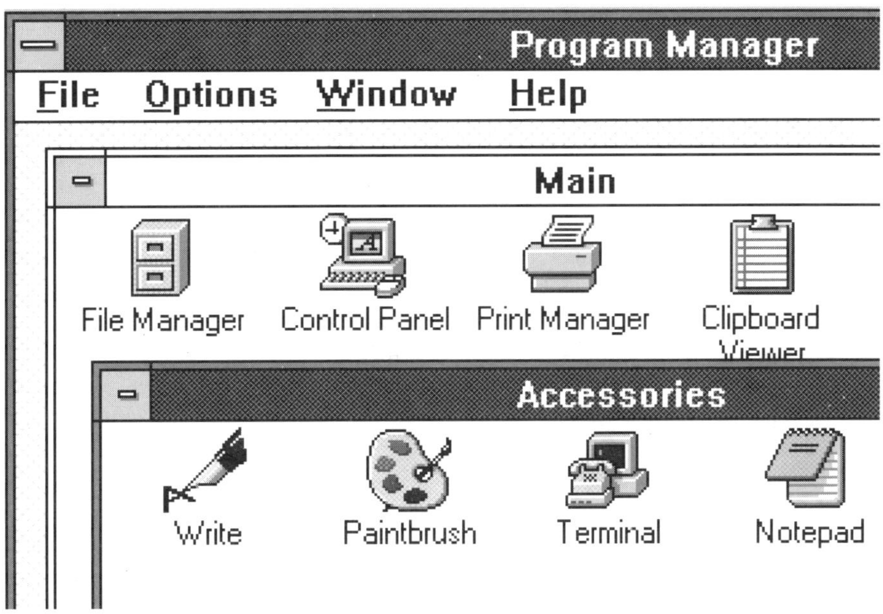

  - icons
    are pictures which are used to represent software. Operations on icons include pointing, clicking and dragging. These control the software.

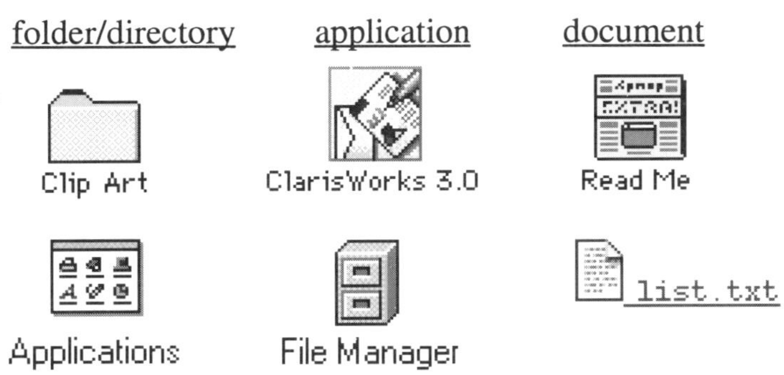

quick check

Low/medium resolution interface - teletext & videotext displays.
High resolution interfaces (icon based interfaces) - windows, icons.

5. High resolution (cont.)

- icon based interfaces (cont.)
  - menus

    A variety of different menu formats exist. In some cases there is no reason why they could not also appear in other, text based HCI systems since they contain only text. If they contain icons or graphics objects then they need high resolution.

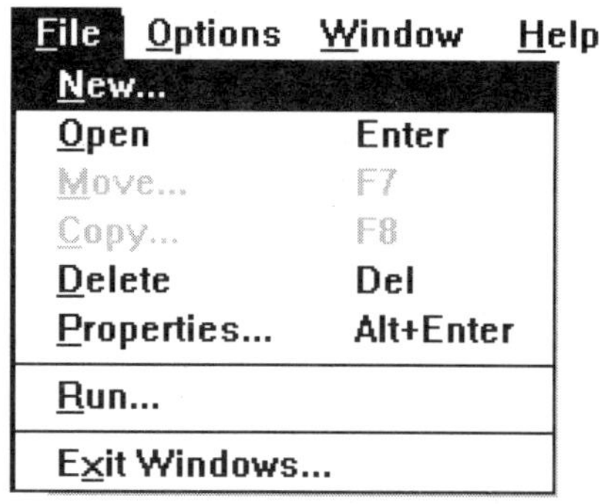

· A drop-down menu appears when the menu is chosen and remains on screen until an option is selected, or the mouse is clicked outside the menu.

· A pull-down menu appears when the menu is chosen and remains on screen as long as the mouse button remains down. To select an item the highlight is dragged down and released when the required option is highlighted.

· An icon-based pull-down menu

  - dialogue boxes

    These can be simple, with little choice, or complex with many possible choices.

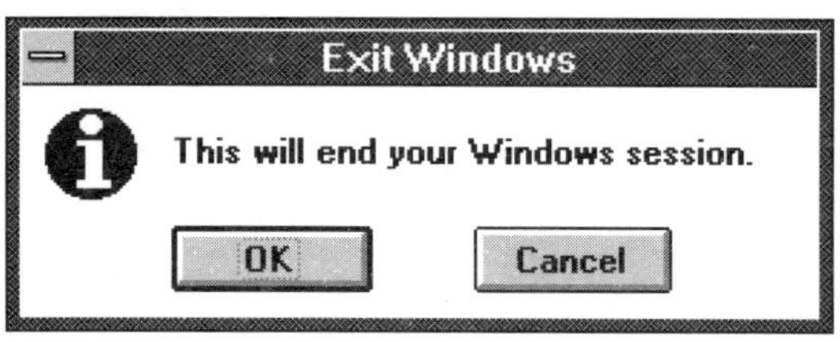

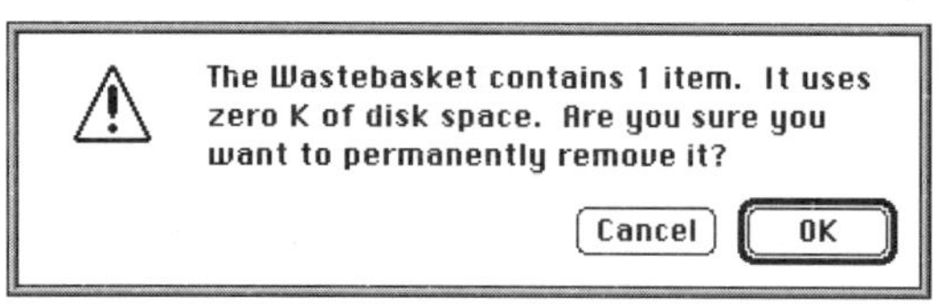

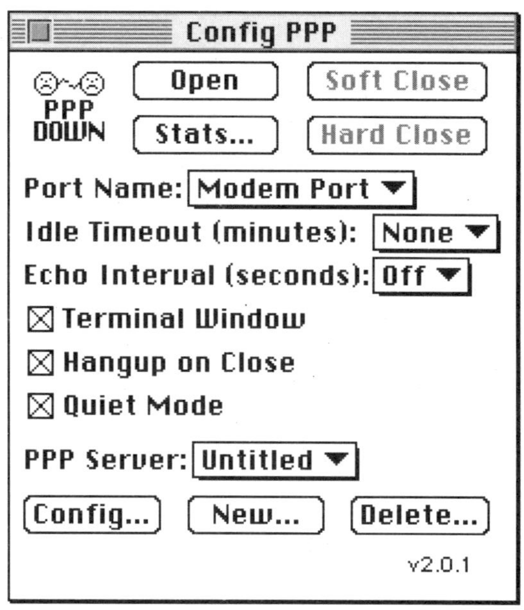

quick check

High Resolution (icon based interfaces) menus, dialogue boxes.

6. Why users like WIMP systems

- keyboarding skills are not important.
- options presented - which do not need to be 'known' - the user can search menus to see what can be done.
- fast presentation and selection of alternatives.
- options are presented textually and graphically.
- less scope for error.

7. Why users DO NOT like WIMP systems

- seen as slow and clumsy - to select menus requires using a mouse so taking hands off keyboard.
- users find the screen cluttered with information rarely used.
- giving textual commands has greater flexibility and allows more complex operations.
- confusion exists when more than one mouse button is available.

8. The desktop metaphor

This describes the way in which a windowing system simulates a conventional desktop. On a desktop papers are laid one on top of another with the document currently in use placed on top. A windowing system lays one window on top of another with the currently used window as the top layer. Just as a desktop can become cluttered with papers, so a windowing system can become cluttered if too many windows are open.

9. Ergonomics

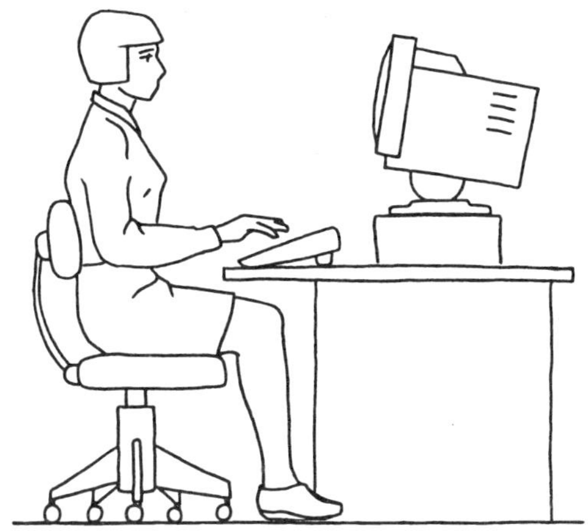

Ergonomics is concerned with the relationship of humans to their working environment. In a computer context this includes such items as the design of keyboards and peripherals, the seating of the user, the organisation of the hardware in use, the angle of the screen, heating (and cooling), lighting and noise levels. In an ideal HCI these will be as important as the ease of use of the software.

10. Future possibilities

Technology is changing constantly. The hardware used in computer systems is operating at faster and faster speeds; the software is becoming ever more complex. One effect on the HCI may be that conventional methods of input and output may give way to more humanised forms. One of the latest effects of this is with handwriting; computers can be trained to recognise handwriting and to convert it to text. Perhaps in the future, as a matter of course, we will tell the computer what to do by talking to it; it will be able to cope with a wide variety of voices and languages. The computer will respond with perfect speech, as well as other appropriate output such as to screen or paper.

quick check

Advantages & disadvantages of WIMP systems. Desktop metaphor. Ergonomics. Future HCIs.

Package Integration

1. Integration of packages

Integration refers to the ease with which different packages can work together. This effectively means consideration of the question 'how easily can data be transferred from one package to another?' Examples of interaction between packages include:

- merging a mailing list from a database into a word-processor (mail merge).
- transferring a table from a spreadsheet into a word-processing document.
- transferring a set of fields from a database into a word-processing document.
- adding pictures from a graphics package to a word-processed document.
- drawing graphics charts from data in a database.

2. Standard data formats

A number of data formats have become standard, making for easier data transfer between packages, for example:

General:	ASCII
Word-processing:	RTF
Databases:	DBF
Spreadsheets:	SYLK
Graphics:	EPS, GIF, TIFF, PICT

3. Separate packages or integrated package?

It is important to distinguish between a separate application package that can be described as one of the recognised GPPs, and an integrated package.

A <u>single GPP</u>, such as a database or word-processor, performs mainly operations associated with that type of package. Modern packages offer a wide range of operations and tend to require appreciable amounts of memory to operate.

An <u>integrated package</u> offers the facilities of several GPPs in one package, typically word-processing, spreadsheets, databases, graphics and communications.

4. Advantages of integrated packages

A number of advantages exist in using an integrated package:

- the overall memory requirements are similar to those of a single GPP and the different parts of the package are all available once it is loaded into memory.
- the way in which similar operations are carried out will be the same in all parts of the package and the menus will be similar in appearance. The syntax is consistent across the parts of the package.
- data is easily transferred from one part of the package to another since it is a format common to the whole integrated package. No data translators are required to change from one data format to another (though the integrated package may allow data to be imported from other packages with different data formats, and exported in those formats).

However, a compromise has to be made, particularly for the whole package to fit into a relatively small amount of memory. The range of operations within any one part of the integrated package is more limited than in a GPP.

5. Static and Dynamic links

Links can be set up between the data in different parts of an integrated package.

If the link is <u>static</u> ('cold link') then the link only exists as the data is being transferred. The link is then broken and any further changes in the original data do not result in a change in the destination data.

A <u>dynamic</u> link ('hot link') between applications will automatically change the destination data if any change is made to the original data.

There are advantages in both situations.

A static link produces a one-off update of data which is then not changed further.

A dynamic link gives an up-to-date copy at all times.

quick check

Package integration. Standard data formats. Separate GPP -v- integrated package. Advantages of integrated package. Static link, dynamic link.

3. Programming

1. Areas of study
Three areas of study are identified when studying programming:

- Programming and problem solving.
- Program design aspects and programming style.
- Programming languages and environments.

Programming and Problem Solving

2. Programming
Programming at Higher Grade is mainly concerned with the use of a High Level Language (HLL) to solve computing problems. You will probably study only one HLL in the time available for the practical part of the course. You must realise that a range of high level languages exist. Each one will have different characteristics and programming environments making it better suited to particular types of problem.

The systematic approach
is recognised as the most effective way of producing a solution. Formalising the process into a set of separate stages is most likely to produce the best solution, free from errors and as required by the end user. This is particularly important in commercial programming environments, where a team of programmers might be working on different parts of a complex program. In amateur situations, programming has often been a series of disjointed pieces of program. Extra parts may have been added on as afterthoughts. The program may solve the problem but is perhaps inefficient in the use of memory or backing storage and is difficult to alter, for example when making changes or correcting errors. The main emphasis in the Higher Grade course is concerned with what a commercial organisation would do.

3. Problem Solving
A number of different stages are involved when developing a solution to problems by using programming languages:

- Problem analysis
- Program design
- Describing the design
- Implementation

The main features of these stages are outlined on the following pages; some are further developed in later sections.

3a. Problem analysis
involves the production of a clear definition of what is required to solve a problem. This usually means a formal **program specification document**, converting the initial description of what the program is to do into a clear, precise and unambiguous statement.

3b. Why specification is important
The specification can form the basis of a legal agreement between client and software company. It is needed because the initial description will often be vague and incomplete. Assumptions will almost certainly have been made which require clarification. The end user and programmer must both be able to understand and agree on the final description, so it must be as clear and concise as possible. Any disagreements about the final program between the parties should be able to be resolved by referring to the document; this is only possible if it is complete and comprehensive.

quick check

Areas of study. Programming, The systematic approach. Problem solving - problem analysis, importance of specification.

4. Program design

This stage takes the program definition and describes the way in which the solution is to be achieved. A variety of methods have been used to achieve this but one commonly used technique is **top-down design**.

4a. Top-down design

The problem is broken down into a relatively small number of subproblems. Each subproblem may subsequently be broken down further. By starting at the top (the whole problem) and going down successively (to smaller problems) the result is a number of small subproblems which are relatively simple to code.
This is also called **step-wise refinement**.

4b. Alternatives to high level languages

It is not always the case that using a high level language is the best solution to a problem. Another route may be either to use a general purpose package as it is, or to use the language provided to customise the GPP to suit the requirements of the problem.

4c. Examples of alternatives

For example, a problem may be simply to do the tasks of a word-processor - to enter, edit, save, retrieve and print text. This would probably be best done using an existing general purpose package. However, the task of scrambling text, using complex algorithms to encrypt it for security reasons, would almost certainly require the use of a programming language.
It is also possible that a problem is not able to be solved by either a GPP or high level language. The only alternative is to move to a lower level of software. This may involve the use of a low level or assembly language.

4d. Module libraries

Some tasks occur often, both within a program and in different programs. Such common tasks are suitable for storing in a library of subprograms which can be extracted and used in new programs. This is at its best when the library module exactly matches the requirements of the problem, but is also of use when it can be tailored by small modifications to suit the task. One consequence of this is that there needs to be an exact description of the module environment to allow the programmer to know whether it is suitable to use.
Using a module library can vary from one language to another. In some cases it may involve typing in the code again - not friendly! In other cases a whole library can be loaded in and may even be regarded as an extension of the language itself. Between these extremes is the situation where the programmer will open up a library of modules, copy the required code and paste it into the program being developed.

4e. Combining partial solutions

Four main methods exist:

- abutment
  one partial solution is added after the other.

- merging
  the partial solutions are interleaved.

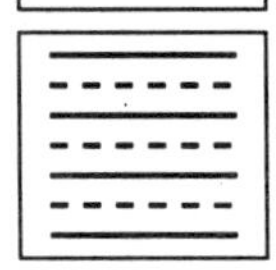

- nesting
  one partial solution is placed entirely within another.

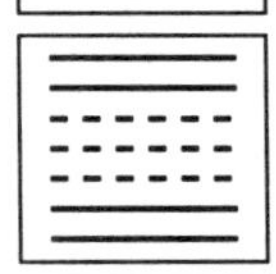

- tailoring
  add a partial solution, with modifications.

quick check

Program design - top-down design, alternatives to HLL, module libraries, combining partial solutions.

5. Describing the design

Several methods are commonly used to describe the design of a program:

- Pseudocode
- Structure diagram or chart
- Flow chart

These are described more fully in the section on program design on page 23.

6. Language constructs

Constructs typical of high level procedural languages are:

- modularity
- statements and control structures
- data types
- expressions
- input/output

These are all described below.

6a. Modularity

is concerned with structures that allow a program to be broken down into separate structures or subprograms. Each of these can be solved on their own and then put together to make the complete program. Typical structures are functions and procedures or subroutines. Data can be exchanged between parts of a program by being passed as parameters.

Procedures are self-contained program structures which can be called from the main program, or from other procedures. They can be called from different parts of the program, thus avoiding code repetition.

Functions are self-contained program structures designed to return a value. High level languages will provide some built-in functions but will also allow you to define your own.

Parameters are the names and values passed to and from procedures and functions. The use of parameters, together with local variables, makes a program less likely to be troubled with errors during execution. Parameters may be passed by value or by reference.

Passing parameters by reference results in manipulation of the actual parameter itself. Even if it is referred to in the subprogram by a different name, any processes are carried out on the original value. Referenced parameters are used when output is required from the subprogram, perhaps when a value is passed in, possibly altered and passed back again to the calling part of the program.

Passing parameters by value results in a local copy in the subprogram of the parameter used in the subprogram call. The subprogram manipulates this local copy and the original is unaffected. Passing parameters in this way is safer to use because accidental changes to values in the calling part of the program are avoided. However, it cannot be used if the changed value is to be passed back to the calling part of the program. Also, if the parameter is a large structure such as an array this results in two copies of the array existing; this has serious memory implications. Some languages will not allow arrays to be passed by value.

Scope of variables - the scope of a variable defines those parts of a program where the variable may be used. Variables may be local or global.

Local variables exist only within subprograms. They can only be used in that procedure or function and have no value outside the subprogram.

Global variables are declared for use throughout the whole program, in the main program block and within any function or procedure. Global variables need to be used with care, since their values can be inadvertently altered within subprograms; this can be difficult to trace.

quick check

Design description. Language constructs; Modularity - procedures, functions, parameters, passing parameters by value and reference, scope of variables, local variables, global variables.

6b. Data types

Within programs data is represented by variables. Various data types exist. It is important to distinguish between the different data types. This is because the operations that can be carried out on them, and the way in which they are stored, depends on the data type. In some languages the data type of each variable has to be specified in data declarations. In others the data type may be defined by the syntax of the name used. Data types discussed here are:

- Integer, real, Boolean, character and string data types.
- One dimensional arrays, records, sequential files.

Integer numbers are whole numbers, both positive and negative, and zero. Storing data as an integer has the advantages of exact representation and fast execution of operations; however, there are system limits on the range that can be stored (for example, between -32768 and +32767).

Real numbers are numbers with a fractional part. In many languages this means a number using floating point storage. There are still system limitations but the range of numbers that can be represented is much larger than with integers. More memory is also required than for integers, and the representation is not exact so errors can occur.

Boolean data type can take two values - TRUE or FALSE. This data type is treated differently by different systems.

Character data type is one of the set of symbols which a computer can represent such as letters, digits and punctuation marks.

Strings are lists of characters grouped together.

Record data types are less commonly supported by languages. They allow different data types to be grouped together and treated as a single unit. An example is pupil information where each name, address, age, admission number and date of birth are handled together.

An **array (one dimensional)** is a set of storage locations referenced by a single name. Each member of the array must be of the same data type and is referred to by a unique identifying subscript. Typical examples are **name$(20)** or **pupil(50)**.

Sequential files require the data to be stored, and retrieved, in sequence. Each data item will be stored one after another. Extra data items can be added at the end of the file. The data items can only be retrieved in the order in which they were stored.

Files are organised sets of related data. For example, this could be the set of records relating to the pupils in a class. These are stored on backing storage for later use. Alternatively it could just be a list of the names of your friends.

quick check

Data types - integer, real number, Boolean, character, string, one-dimensional array, record, sequential file.

6c. Input/Output

Program input may come from a variety of sources, such as a keyboard, mouse, joystick, or sensor. Output may be to screen, printer, plotter or motor. In addition, backing storage, network interfaces, modems and other devices can be involved with both input and output. Programming structures must exist to allow the system to distinguish what devices are intended to be used with a particular input/output command. Some languages only allow input/output to be done via files of data.

Input from a keyboard may require a single character or a string of characters. Most high level languages have commands to deal with either situation. In the former case, program execution halts until a key is pressed; the key value is assigned to some variable and execution continues. In the latter case, a buffer stores the keys pressed until a specific key indicates entry is complete (e.g. the return key). The buffer contents are then stored in a variable and program execution recommences.
Other forms of input come from other interfaces which may be required to identify themselves. This is typically done either through the assignment of channel numbers to identify specific interfaces or through the use of specialised commands for different interfaces.

Output is normally to the screen but different output devices are selected in much the same way as for input devices; either channel numbers or special commands in the language decide where output is to be sent.

End detection - during input/output processes it is sometimes not clear when the process has to end. For example, reading in data from a sequential file on backing storage. The length of the file is not fixed and will vary if items are added to it or deleted from it. What is required is a structure in the language which allows data to be read from the file until the end is reached. Without this facility, further efforts to read from the file may result in an execution error.

6d. Statements and control structures

Assignment is concerned with the allocation of values to variables.

Sequence is the placement of instructions or subproblems (functions or procedures) in order, one after another.

Selection is the process of testing to see whether a condition is true. If this is so then some action is executed. Selection may be a simple case of only one condition to test; it may have two possible conditions to test, each with their associated resultant action; there may be multiple conditions to test, with a corresponding number of possible actions.

Repetition is the process of carrying out one or more instructions repeatedly. At some point a condition must be tested to see whether the repetition is to continue. This is also known as looping. Three types of loop are identified:

- fixed loops - for a specified number of repetitions.
- pre-indexed loops where the loop is entered only if a condition is met.
- post-indexed loops which are executed at least once and then repeated if a condition is met.

Calls to procedures are made from the main program or from within subprograms. This is done by the name of the procedure and may involve the passing of parameters.

quick check

Input, output, end detection.
Statements and control structures - assignment, sequence, selection, repetition, procedure calls.

6e. Expressions

A number of different expressions can be identified. They are operations which evaluate a value as a result of some process.

Arithmetical expressions operate on numerical data and use arithmetic operators such as +, -, / and *.

String expressions operate on strings. The main processes involve slicing (the result is a new string formed from a part of the original) or concatenation (making a larger string from smaller ones joined together).

Function calls are expressions which allocate a value to a variable as a result of operations carried out within the function. Parameters may or may not be passed to the function.

Comparison involves two items of data of the same data type. The action taken depends on whether the result is TRUE or FALSE. This occurs, for example, in selection statements or in a loop to determine whether repetition is to continue.

Logical expressions produce Boolean variables as a result of some operation, for example:

```
LET pass = mark >= 50
```

could result in pass being TRUE if the value of mark is 50 or greater.

7. Common algorithms

These algorithms (in pseudocode) are typical of subprograms found in module libraries.

7a. Count occurrences

This will go through a list of items and count the number of times the loop is executed.

```
set counter to zero
begin loop
    get an item of data
    increase counter by 1
end loop
```

7b. Maximum/minimum

The largest and smallest value in a list are determined.

```
get an item of data
set min and max to data item
begin loop
    get an item of data
    if data greater than max then
            set max to data
    end if
    if data is less than min then
            set min to data
    end if
end loop
```

7c. Frequency count

The number of occurrences of a target item in a list is counted.

```
set counter to zero
begin loop
    get an item of data
    if data matches target item then
            increase counter by 1
    end if
end loop
```

7d. Searching and sorting

A number of other common algorithms exist for the processes of searching, sorting and list maintenance. The main features are summarised on the next page, but you should refer to other sources for the associated algorithms. The algorithm selected to carry out any particular task depends on the requirements of the problem.

quick check

Expressions - arithmetical, string, function calls, comparisons, logical.
Algorithms - count occurrences, maximum/minimum, frequency count, searching & sorting.

7e. Searching

is the process of locating a record in a file using the item (or key) to be located. A number of algorithms exist for searching, including:

- linear (or sequential) search
- binary search
- tree search

Only the first two are required.

Linear search
This is a relatively slow type of search, suitable for all lists. A list is searched, starting at the beginning, going from item to item until the target item is located or the end of the list is reached. If the target is found, the search returns the location of the item. On average, the number of comparisons for a list of n items is $\frac{(n+1)}{2}$.

Binary search
This is a relatively fast search, suitable only for ordered lists. It assumes the list is sorted in a specified order (ascending or descending). After each comparison the size of the list is reduced by half. The maximum number of comparisons for a list of n items is $\log_2(n)$.

7f. Sorting

involves putting lists of data into some predetermined order. The lists of data can be **external** or **internal**.

- External sorting is used when the list is too large to fit in the memory. The whole list is divided into several smaller sub-lists and is held on backing storage. Each sub-list is loaded into memory, sorted and stored on backing storage. The sub-lists are then merge sorted to produce the whole sorted list.
- Internal sorting holds the entire list in the memory of the computer. A variety of different internal sorting techniques exist. The one which is most suitable is determined by the nature of the problem.

The various sort categories include:

- selection sort
- exchange sort (bubble sort)
- tree sort
- insertion sort
- shell sort
- quick sort (partition sort)

Selection sort
This is a simple sort which maintains two lists - the original list and a sorted list. The original list is scanned to find the smallest item which is placed in the first available position in the sorted list.

Exchange sort
This sort allows the sorted item to rise through the list, hence the alternative name. Pairs of data items are compared, one after another, and exchanged if necessary to put them in the correct order. After each pass through the list at least one item is in its correct position.

7g. Maintaining lists

Processes include adding, deleting and amending items in the list.

Adding to a list
When adding an item to a list the usual method is to append the new item to the end of the list, then sort it into order if required.

Deleting from a list
When deleting an item from a list the item may or may not be at the end of the list. If it is not at the end then all items below are first moved up one place (so overwriting the item). In either case the list length is then reduced by one.

quick check

Searching - linear search, binary search.
Sorting - selection sort, exchange sort. Adding an item to a list, deleting an item from a list.

8. Documentation

Documentation for programs comes in a variety of forms, though not all programs will have all types of documentation produced for them. The two main types are:

- program documentation
- user documentation

8a. Program documentation

This includes:

- the program specification document (see page 15)
- the program design (for example, algorithm, structure diagram or flow chart, see page 23)
- complete program listing
- sample output from the program
- suitable test data including:
  - valid data within acceptable limits;
  - valid data at the limits;
  - data outwith the limits (including zero, negative numbers and empty strings).

8b. User documentation

This includes:

- internal commentary (part of the program listing)
- user guide (manual). This may include:
  - a description of how to install the program;
  - how to use the program;
  - reference material;
  - tutorial material.

Program Design Aspects and Programming Style

1. Program design

This stage in program development follows on from the problem analysis. A solution is planned taking into account the contents of the program specification document. A number of objectives should be met in designing a solution; in general terms the software produced should be:

Correct
Correct programs meet the program specification.

Reliable
Reliable programs are free from errors of coding or design and work properly for all specified inputs.

Maintainable
Maintainable programs can be easily and quickly changed at some later stage.

Readable
Readable programs can be easily understood by other programmers, and by the original programmer at a later stage.

Portable
Portable programs can be relatively easily amended to run on a computer system for which they were not originally designed.

Efficient
Efficient programs make effective use of memory and storage facilities and operate at an acceptable speed.

quick check

Documentation - program documentation, user documentation.
Program design - correctness, reliability, maintainability, readability, portability, efficiency.

2. Describing the program design

The program design is a set of instructions describing the steps in solving a problem. It is commonly known as an **algorithm**. Three main methods are used to describe the design of a program:

2a. Flow charts

This is the traditional method of expressing an algorithm. Flow charts can easily become complicated for anything other than simple programs. Boxes are used to contain the description of each step; special shapes are used to distinguish different processes.

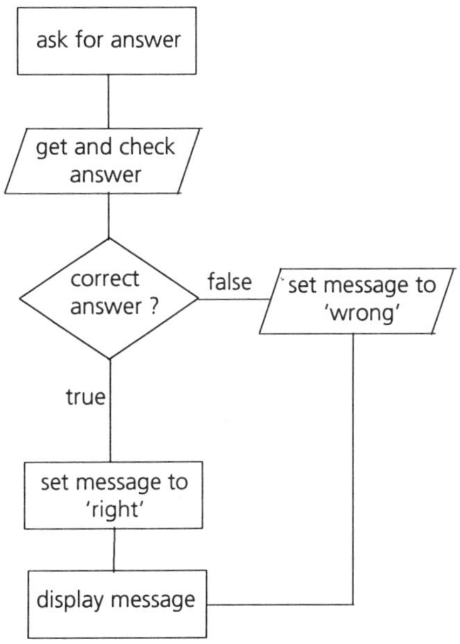

2b. Structure diagrams

This diagrammatic algorithm emphasises the top-down structured approach to programming. Levels of sub-tasks are identified; they must be completed before control is passed back to the level above. The self-contained nature of sub-tasks will allow them to be coded and tested independently of the rest of the program.

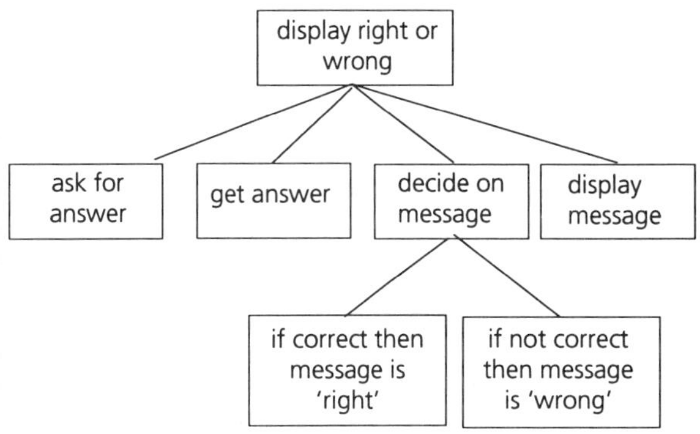

2c. Pseudocode

This is a code which describes the program design in English-like text; it may appear to be similar to some programming languages. It is best described as a code somewhere between English and a programming language. There is no standard pseudocode; what is important is that the meaning is clear to the programmers who use it. Indentation is often used to aid clarity, as in a programming language.

<u>main algorithm</u>

```
1       ask for answer
2       get and check answer
3       display message
```

<u>Refine step 2</u>

```
2.1     get answer
2.2     if answer correct then
2.3         set message to 'right'
2.4     else
2.5         set message to 'wrong'
2.6     end if
```

quick check

Describing the program design, algorithms - flow charts, structure diagrams, pseudocode.

3. Programming style

Professional programmers develop a style, both in the way in which they design programs and in the various aspects of the human-computer interface of their products. Within a company the programmers will know the in-house preferences; new employees will be expected to follow the same style. Most individual programmers working alone develop their own particular styles in their work.

3a. Design styles

The adoption of standard design styles aids both the readability and maintainability of programs. It will be affected by local circumstances, including the systems in use, the methods previously used and the languages supported. This may involve the:

- design methods adopted (e.g. top-down)
- use of module libraries
- input and output structures
- use of parameters
- balance of local and global variables
- names used for variables, procedures and functions
- internal documentation included
- style of format of program such as spacing and indentation.

3b. User interface styles

Features which may affect the user interface include:

- Start up procedures
  These should be simple to execute and as automated as possible.
- Robustness of software
  Any potential sources of error should be anticipated and avoided where possible. User input should be echoed to the screen and validated by the software. Users should be informed of any unacceptable input. Defensive programming techniques should be used.
- Presentation
  The screen layout should be clear and easy to understand. Graphics and colour should be used sensibly, avoiding excess. Similar operations should be carried in a consistent manner. The facility of checking actions before they are carried out avoids frustrations although if used excessively it is annoying. Output should have a sensible format. Help facilities should be available where necessary. Menus, of whatever kind, help the user know which options are available.

4. Errors

Programming errors may be:

- run-time errors
  occur during program execution and cause unexpected termination.
- logical errors
  are mistakes in programming and cause unexpected results.
- syntax errors
  result from incorrect use of the language and are detected by the translator.

5. Defensive programming

aims to avoid errors, for example:

- all input is validated
- local variables are used
- programs are tested extensively
- possible sources of errors are anticipated
- typical run-time errors are avoided:
  - numbers going out of range
  - division by zero
  - array subscripts too large
  - reading past the end of data or a file
  - case statement not matching labels.

quick check

Programming styles - design, user interface.
Errors. Defensive programming.

Programming Languages and Environments

1. Levels of language

A hierarchy of levels of language can be identified:

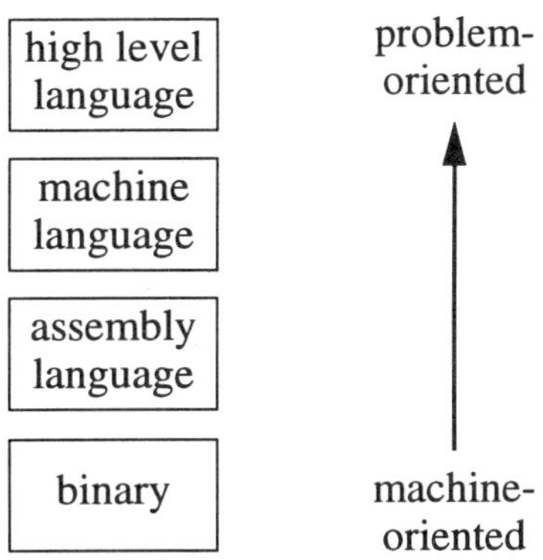

2. High Level Languages

A number of features are typical of high level languages:

- they are problem-oriented.
- each instruction may be equivalent to several machine language instructions. This makes programs shorter than those at a lower level.
- programs are portable. With relatively little adaptation needed they can run on different machines, using translators written specifically for that machine.

3. Classification of languages

There are several ways in which high level languages can be classified:

- according to the **purposes** for which they were developed
- according to the **structure** of the language

- **Classification by purpose**

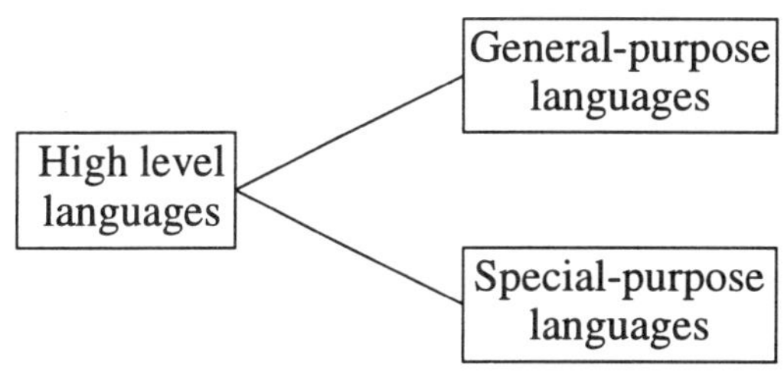

  - General purpose languages are designed as universal languages, not restricted to one main use but able to cope with a range of programming problems. Some general purpose languages are large (many reserved words) and so more difficult to learn.

    For example: PL/1, ALGOL 68

  - Special purpose languages are designed for limited applications and may not be capable of performing operations required by particular problems.

    For example:

commerce	COBOL
science	FORTRAN
education	PASCAL
industry	APT
AI	PROLOG

    Some special purpose languages have evolved to become general purpose. Also, some general purpose languages have mainly been used in specialist areas and are often seen to be special purpose. The distinction between general and special purpose is relative. It is, to some extent, an outdated distinction.

    For example: BASIC, FORTH and LOGO are often described as special purpose, but it could be argued that they are general purpose.

quick check

Levels of language. High level languages. Classification of languages - by purpose.

3. Classification of languages (cont.)

- **Classification by structure**

By looking at the structure of languages a number of different classifications can be identified. For example:

◦ high level or low level?		i.e. problem-oriented or machine-oriented?
	or	machine independent or machine dependent?
		e.g. BASIC or 68000 assembly language
◦ interpreted or compiled?		e.g. Turbo PASCAL or BBC BASIC
◦ structured or unstructured?	i.e.	divided into subproblems or not divided?
		e.g. ALGOL or COBOL
◦ numeric or symbolic?	i.e.	based on numbers or symbols/graphics?
		e.g. FORTRAN or LISP/LOGO
◦ imperative or declarative?		i.e. procedural or non-procedural?
	or	prescriptive or descriptive
		user specifies steps or does not specify steps
		e.g. COMAL or PROLOG

Not all languages can be easily placed in any particular classification and some can be used in either of the extremes depending on circumstances.

4. Primitives

are the core vocabulary of some languages. They are language building blocks - commands or operations which initiate processes that are determined by the language.

New primitives or procedures can be created using the existing vocabulary. They can then be used as if they had always been a part of the language.

5. Choosing which language to use

The programmer is not solely concerned with the various features of languages which affect their suitability for a particular task. A number of languages might be contenders. The final choice may yet be affected by other considerations such as:

- the programmer's expertise in particular languages.
- which languages are available to the programmer.
- the software development environments of the languages.

6. Software development environment

This describes the presence and quality of various features of a language (the development tools) which help with the production of the program, for example:

- ease of use of translators
  for example, compiled languages must be compiled before execution whereas interpreted languages are not.
- error handling and reporting
  how a program behaves when an error occurs; whether it 'hangs up' or provides the user with a full description of the problem, both at translation and at run-time. The process of removing errors is called 'debugging the program'.
- structured listings
  producing a listing with indentation and automatic capitalisation of keywords.
- editors
  text editors to enter and edit the source programs and linkage editors to add material from module libraries, either compiled or not.
- trace facilities
  tracing through the program step by step showing the changes to output and variables.

quick check

Classification of languages - by structure,
Primitives. Choosing which language to use. Software development environment.

4. Computer Systems

Low level machine

Data Representation

Computers store three main types of data: numbers, text and graphics.

1. **'Number crunching'** was one of the first uses of computers and their ability to perform very complex calculations at high speeds remains one of their main uses. **Text processing** is also a major function of computers. From the storage of vast quantities of names and addresses in large databases to using a word-processor, text handling is of vital importance to today's computers. **Storage of graphics** has more recently become important because of the widespread use of desktop publishing and computer-aided design.

2. **How the computer stores numbers**
Numbers in a computer are stored in binary using only the digits 0 and 1. These binary digits each represent a power of two. Starting at the right of a number, the first digit shows how many units the number contains. The next digit to the left shows the number of twos; then fours, eights, sixteens etc. This is best shown by a diagram:

place value	8	4	2	1
binary number	1	1	1	0

This represents the decimal number 14.
This is calculated as:
$$1*8 + 1*4 + 1*2 + 0*1 = 14$$
When there are more binary digits, the one at the right always has the value one:

place value	128	64	32	16	8	4	2	1
binary number	1	1	1	0	0	1	1	1

This represents the decimal number 231.
This is calculated as:
$1*128 + 1*64 + 1*32 + 1*4 + 1*2 + 1*1$

A binary number with 4 bits can represent decimal numbers in the range 0 to 15.

A binary number with 8 bits can represent decimal numbers in the range 0 to 255.

3. **Conversion from binary to decimal**
is achieved by writing down column headings above the binary digits and adding up the powers of 2 where a 1 occurs.
For example, to convert 1101 to decimal

8	4	2	1	
1	1	0	1	= 8 + 4 + 1 = 13

4. **Conversion from decimal to binary**
is achieved by repeatedly dividing the decimal number by 2 until 0 is obtained and writing down the remainder each time.
For example, to convert 14 to binary

2	14	
2	7	r 0
2	3	r 1
2	1	r 1
	0	r 1

By reading up the digits of the remainder the answer 1110 is obtained.

5. **Rules for binary addition**
There are only three rules required for adding binary numbers. These are shown below:
$0 + 0 = 0$
$1 + 0 = 1$ (or $0 + 1 = 1$)
$1 + 1 = 0$ (with a carry of 1)

6. **Positive and negative integers**
There are two main methods of representing integers (whole numbers) in a computer so that both positive and negative numbers can be shown. The left digit is used as a sign bit.

- The simplest method is **sign and magnitude**. The sign bit is 1 for negative and 0 for positive. The rest of the digits show the magnitude of the number.
For example, to show both +5 and -5 as 8-bit binary numbers using this method:
+5 = 0000 0101   -5 = 1000 0101
In each case the left-most bit is the sign bit, the other seven digits represent the value 5.

quick check
Low level machine, data representation. Number crunching. How the computer stores numbers. Conversion binary-decimal, decimal-binary. Rules for binary addition. Sign and magnitude for integers.

6. Positive and negative integers (cont.)

- The second method of representing negative numbers is **two's complement**. Calculating a two's complement involves inverting all the bits of a binary number (to find the one's complement) then adding 1.

For example, to find the two's complement of the number: **0101**

invert all the digits to find the one's complement: **1010**

then add 1 **1011**

Using two's complement the sign bit is **1** for negative and **0** for positive. In a positive number the remaining bits show the size of the number but in a negative number they show the two's complement. Using the same examples as before, +5 and -5 in 8-bit notation would be shown as:

+5 = 0000 0101 -5 = 1111 1011

Note that positive numbers are the same using the sign and magnitude or two's complement method but negative numbers are different.

sign & mag	2's complement
+5 = 0000 0101	0000 0101
-5 = 1000 0101	1111 1011

7. Floating point representation

Computers can store very large numbers. To do this, they may have to lose some accuracy. The numbers are stored in **floating point** format. For example, a decimal number such as 123456789 can be shown as the two numbers 0.123456789×10^9.

The number 0.123456789 is the **mantissa** and the number 9 is the **exponent**.

The numbers stored in the computer are, of course, binary numbers. A binary number stored in floating point form might be:

$$1001011010010110 \times 2^{10010110}$$

The same system is used to store non-integer (real) numbers.

8. Fixed point representation

Fractions can be expressed in binary by extending the binary concepts seen above. In this case the digits after the point represent $\frac{1}{2}, \frac{1}{4}, \frac{1}{8}$ etc.

A **fixed-point** number is one which is represented by a set of digits with the point in the correct position. For example:

145.343 is a fixed point decimal number.
1101.101 is a fixed point binary number.

9. Most and least significant bit

The most significant bit (msb) in a binary number is that on the left-hand side of the number. The least significant bit (lsb) is that on the right-hand side of the number:

msb—— 1111 1011 ——— lsb

10. Most significant bit in 2's complement

The most significant bit in a two's complement representation of a number represents the place value as a negative number. The remaining bits in the number represent the positive place values. For example, the number 11111011 is explained as:

1	1 1 1 1 0 1 1
-128	+ 64 + 32 + 16 + 8 + 2 + 1 = -5

11. Why use 2's complement

There are advantages in using 2's complement rather than signed bit because:

- signed bit has 2 values for zero, +0 and -0
- signed bit does not always give a logical sequence of numbers when adding 1 to a number.

12. Why computers use binary

There are advantages in using binary in computers because:

- switches are set on and off to match binary values of 1 and 0
- the rules of binary arithmetic are simple
- with only two levels for 1 and 0, electrical variations are less important.

quick check

Two's complement for integers. Floating point representation, fixed point representation.
Most and least significant bit, msb in two's complement. Why use two's complement. Why computers use binary.

13. Hexadecimal (hex) numbers

Another number base associated with computers is hexadecimal (base 16).
This is shown by either the letters hex or the symbol &.
For example, &FE is hex number FE.

denary (base 10)	hexadecimal (base 16)	binary (base 2)
1	1	0001
2	2	0010
3	3	0011
4	4	0100
5	5	0101
6	6	0110
7	7	0111
8	8	1000
9	9	1001
10	A	1010
11	B	1011
12	C	1100
13	D	1101
14	E	1110
15	F	1111
16	10	10000

14. Reasons for using hex

Numbers are shorter and easier to remember and enter than their binary equivalents. They also take less room to display. It is easy to convert from binary to hex and back again since hex digits may be translated singly into their binary equivalents.
For example, &FE is 1111(F) 1110(E).
1 byte is stored as 2 hex digits.

Changing from base 10 to hex is accomplished in a manner similar to the binary conversion shown on page 27 - successive division by 16 then reading the remainders.
In hex to decimal conversion the column headings will be:

4096 (16^3) **256** (16^2) **16** (16^1) and **1** (16^0)

15. How the computer stores text

Text includes all the letters of the alphabet (both capital and small letters); punctuation marks (.,;:? etc.); arithmetic symbols (+-*/ etc.); numbers (if they are not to be used for calculations). A number (binary) is used to represent each character. This number is in a series called ASCII (American Standard Code for Information Interchange). ASCII codes are normally in the decimal range 32 to 127.
One byte can be used to store any one character. Here are some ASCII codes and the characters they represent:

code	character
65	A
99	c
50	2
43	+

16. Character sets

Each ASCII code represents a different character. The group of characters described by a range of ASCII codes is called a **character set**. There are different character sets because different countries use different characters. Also, some character sets may contain graphic characters rather than letters, numbers, punctuation and mathematical symbols.
By allocating 8 bits to an ASCII code there is room for 256 different characters (2^8). This is more than enough for most purposes.

17. Control characters

The normal range of ASCII codes is from 32 to 127. The codes from 0 to 31 are control codes. These are not used as data but instead control operating functions both within the computer and when communicating between different computers. They are non-printing (they will not appear on the screen or as printed output).

quick check

Hexadecimal numbers, reasons for using hex.
How text is stored, character sets, control characters.

18. Graphic Representation

Pictures on computers are usually based on a grid of dots. The more dots there are the better the quality of the image (the higher the resolution). Although most screen images are made up of dots, the images can be stored in different ways.

19. Bit-Mapped Graphics

The simplest way to store a monochrome image is to use a bit-mapped representation. Here the dots or pixels (picture elements) are stored in a 2-dimensional binary array with a one-to-one mapping between the pixels and the bits.

Here is a simple bit-mapped graphic:

By choosing a small part and enlarging it the pixels making it up can be seen. Each would be stored as a 1 (on) or a 0 (off).

The storage requirement for this is easily calculated. The total number of pixels needed is height x width. As one bit is needed per pixel this is also the number of bits. So dividing by 8 gives the number of bytes. For example, for a display 640 x 320:

640 x 320 = 204800 bits
204800 ÷ 8 = 25600 bytes = 25 Kb

20. Resolution

Sometimes the resolution is given in dots per inch (dpi) instead of pixels. For example, a Macintosh Plus has a screen resolution of 72 dpi. So to store an image which is 2 x 1 inches at this resolution would require:

2 x 72 x 72 = 10368 pixels / bits
10368 ÷ 8 = 1296 bytes = 1.27 Kb

The higher the resolution (the more dots per inch), the greater the memory requirements. So to store the same 2 x 1 inch image at typical laser printer (300 dpi) resolution would need:

2 x 300 x 300 = 180000 bits
180000 ÷ 8 = 22500 bytes = 22 Kb

21. Colour and shades of grey

Colour images are stored in a similar way. However, depending on the choice of colours (or grey shades) available, more bits are needed to represent the image. There must be a binary combination to match each different colour. For example,

colours	bits	power of 2	values
2	1	2^1	0, 1
4	2	2^2	00, 01, 10, 11
8	3	2^3	etc.
16	4	2^4	

22. Object Oriented Graphics

Objects are stored with their **attributes**. The computer is aware of the type of shape being displayed and is therefore able to resize it more accurately. This storage method will also benefit when printers with higher resolutions are used to produce better quality images. Typical attributes stored for a circle could be:

circle,centreX,centreY,radius line,fill,pen

or for a line:

line,startX,startY,endX,endY,line,fill,pen

quick check

Graphical representation. Bit-mapped graphics. Resolution. Colour and shades of grey. Object oriented graphics.

Computer Structure

1. Block diagram

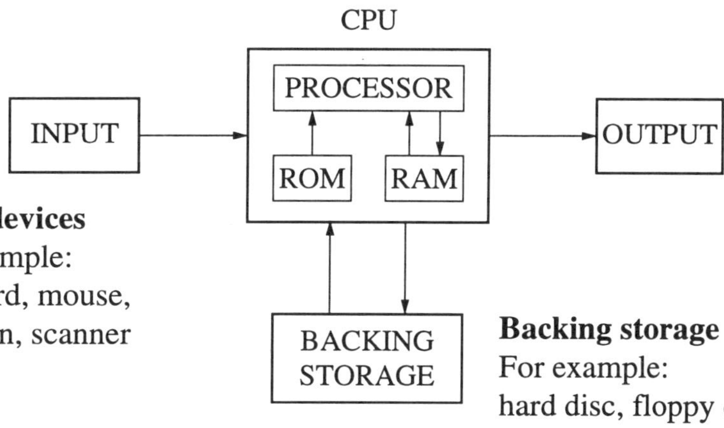

Input devices
For example:
keyboard, mouse, light pen, scanner

Output devices
For example:
monitor, printer, plotter, speaker, motor

Backing storage media
For example:
hard disc, floppy disc, optical disc, CD-ROM

2. Bus structure

- A bus is a group of parallel wires, one for each bit of a word, along which bits of data can flow as electrical signals.
- Buses are used to connect components together.
- Some buses are **bidirectional** allowing data to flow in either direction.
- Buses may be dedicated to one function or may carry data for different functions.
- Buses may be **internal** (for example, between CPU and registers) or **external** (for example, between CPU and other peripherals).
- Bus width determines the length of a word which it can handle at any one time.

3. Bus types

Most computers have three main buses. These are the **data bus, address bus** and **control bus**.
Others may exist, such as a separate Input/Output bus, but these three are the most common.

4. The data bus

is a bidirectional bus carrying data and instructions from memory to the CPU and data from the CPU to memory. This data may be instructions (in machine code), ASCII codes (e.g. representing text), numbers or graphic data.

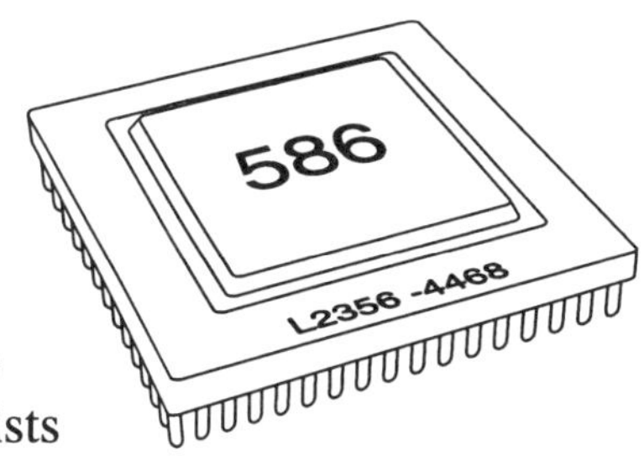

On an older system such as the BBC containing a 6502 processor, the data bus consists of 8 lines (numbered D0 to D7). More modern processors may contain 16 lines (for example, the 68000 or 8086 processors), 32 lines (the 68030 or 486 processors), 64 lines (the Pentium and PowerPC 601 processors) or more.

quick check

Computer structure. Bus structure. Bus types. Data bus.

5. The address bus

is a unidirectional bus carrying the addresses where data or instructions may be found, or should be stored, from the processor to memory. Since the processor requires access to any memory location, each must have a unique identifier (an address) in order that the processor may locate it when required. The size of the address bus must therefore relate directly to the maximum numbers of addresses within any computer, and also therefore to the size of its RAM and ROM.

If an address bus consists of 16 lines, the processor may access 2^{16} different addresses (= 65536). This gives 64 Kb and was the memory size of several of the older 8-bit micros. Newer processors may have 24, 32 or even bigger address buses. A 32-bit address bus would allow access to 2^{32} (= 4294967296) different locations which is 4 gigabytes of memory.

6. The control bus

is different to the other two buses in that, although it is a collection of lines in the same way as they are, these lines are totally unrelated. In the address and data buses, the lines all form part of the same information. In the control bus they are simply grouped together for convenience. Each has a different function and may be used at different times. The purpose of the control lines varies from processor to processor but common processes are:

- **read** to initiate a memory read operation
- **write** to initiate a memory write operation
- **reset** clears all internal registers and starts executing instructions from a pre-defined address (similar to switching off and on again)
- **NMI** The non-maskable interrupt is similar to normal interrupts but cannot be ignored by the processor. This is used for priority interrupts such as imminent power failure.

7. Other control lines

- **clock** carries a signal from the clock chip. In order to synchronize the operations of the processor, a clock generates regular 'pulses' at a rate of between 2 and 100 million per second. These are usually quoted in MHz (million cycles per second). For example, a 25 MHz processor operates with a clock running at 25 million pulses per second. Many processor events are timed to occur within one clock cycle but more complex instructions may take two to four cycles to occur. Modern processors can now operate at speeds of 100 MHz and beyond, meaning that 100 million one-cycle instructions can be performed every second!
- **interrupt** carries a signal to the processor from a peripheral device, which causes it to stop what it is doing (interrupt), save its current status in a special area of memory called the stack, and service the interrupt (for example, printer out of paper - send message to user). It will return to its previous state on completion of this task.

8. Memory read and write

The two basic operations involving the data and address buses are (for 8-bit microprocessors):

- **read from memory** when instructions are fetched or data is read. The steps involved are:
  - CPU sets up 16 address lines with required address;
  - CPU activates read line on control bus;
  - Memory releases data from location onto the data bus.

- **write to memory** when data is sent to memory. The steps are:
  - CPU sets up 16 address lines with required address;
  - CPU sets up 8 data lines with data to be written;
  - CPU activates write line on control bus;
  - data is transferred from the CPU to the memory location.

quick check

Address bus. Control bus, control lines. Memory read and write.

Processor Structure and Instructions

1. Overview

A more detailed look at the CPU shows three main components:
Registers, ALU and Control Unit. These are connected to the rest of the computer via the buses discussed earlier.

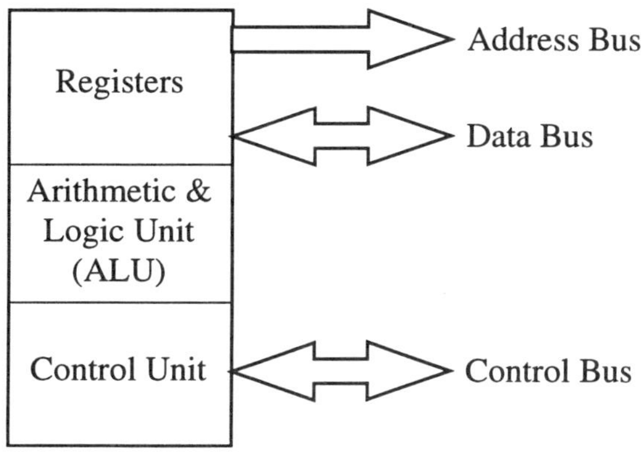

2. The Registers

The processor requires fast access to temporary storage locations for use when setting up buses and fetching instructions, therefore special areas called **registers** exist within the processor itself. The types and number of registers vary greatly from processor to processor but there are certain features common to all of them.

3. Registers <u>not</u> available to programmer

- Memory address register (**MAR**) - contains the address of the data being accessed in main memory. It is directly connected to the address bus.
- Memory data register (**MDR**) - holds the contents of the last selected word written to, or read from, main memory. It is directly connected to the data bus.
- [Current] Instruction Register (**CIR**) or simply (**IR**). When an item of data is identified as an instruction, it is transferred to the IR prior to being decoded and executed.

4. Registers which may be available to the programmer

- Program counter or sequence control register (**PC**) - holds the address of the next instruction to be fetched. After an instruction has been fetched, the PC is automatically incremented by one (sometimes more). It is also altered by certain types of instruction (jumps). It can be altered by the programmer to start program execution from a different address.
- Stack pointer (**SP**) - when a processor is operating, it often needs to use its registers. If the contents of these are to be required at a later date, they must be saved to avoid being overwritten. A special area of memory called the **stack** is used for this. It works on a LIFO (last in first out) principle and the top of the stack is always moving as items are added (pushed) or removed (popped). The SP contains the current position of the top of the stack.

5. Registers available to programmer

- Accumulator (**A**) - so called because it accumulates totals. This is the main general purpose or workhorse register. In many processors all the arithmetic instructions make use of this.
- Other general purpose registers - the number, type and purpose of these varies greatly from processor to processor. There are typically between 2 and 16 in a CISC processor (see page 52 for info. on RISC) and they are used often in data transfers.
- Status register (**SR**) - the bits in the status register are not directly related. To make sense they must be viewed singly. They are flags to signal whether or not certain events have occurred within the processor, for example:
  - a **carry flag** - indicates a carry from a sum in the accumulator.
  - a **minus flag** - the result of the last operation was negative.
  - a **zero flag** - the result of the last operation was zero.

quick check

*Processor structure and instructions. Overview.
Registers, availability to programmers.*

6. The Arithmetic & Logic Unit (ALU)
performs arithmetic functions such as add and subtract, and logical operations such as AND, OR and NOT.

7. The Control Unit
sends control signals thus controlling the operation of all hardware, including I/O devices, and the CPU. It performs this function by fetching, interpreting, and executing each instruction in turn.

8. Fetch - decode - execute cycle

fetch phase:
- contents of PC copied into MAR thus setting up address bus
- PC is incremented
- instruction word transferred from MDR to IR

execute phase:
- instruction in IR decoded
- instruction in IR executed
- unless instruction is STOP, cycle is repeated

9. Instruction format
A machine code instruction comprises two parts:
- the **operation code (op-code)** which is the actual instruction itself (e.g. add, subtract, jump)
- the **operand** which is the source of the data the op-code has to work on. Sometimes the data is implied by the op-code itself (e.g. set carry flag). No further data is required. Sometimes the operand is the data itself, or it may hold the address where the data is stored.

In general, an instruction is written as:

Op code	operand

The op-code tells the processor which **operation** to choose from its instruction set whereas the operand tells it the **object(s)** to be worked on.

10. Instruction length
At the design stage decisions have to be made regarding the size of the instruction set in a processor.
If a processor used 8 bits to represent the op-code, this would allow 256 (2^8) different combinations. If 16 bits were used for each address, this would allow 65536 (2^{16}) or 64 Kb addressable locations.

Assuming that the op-code is 8 bits (1 byte) long, the actual length of any instruction depends on what length of operand is permitted. It may be restricted to one 16-bit address, which would make a total length of 24 (8-bit op-code + 16-bit operand) or it may allow two, three or even more addresses per instruction.

For example, if the processor had to add the contents of two addresses and store the answer in a third, it could be done as follows:

In a **three address** instruction:

8 bits	16 bits	16 bits	16 bits
ADD	**A1**	**A2**	**A3**

This requires only one instruction but occupies 56 bits.

In a **two address** instruction, two instructions will be needed:

ADD A1 A2 (40 bits)
MOVE A2 A3 (40 bits)

Finally a **one address** instruction gives:

LOAD A1 (24 bits)
ADD A2 (24 bits)
STORE A3 (24 bits)

Since longer instructions are more complex and therefore require more clock cycles per instruction, the design engineer must agree a compromise for any particular processor.

quick check

ALU. Control unit. Fetch-decode-execute cycle.
Instruction format. Instruction length.

11. Instruction types

All the commands available within any processor are called its **instruction set**. Most computers have four main types of instruction shown here (with examples in brackets):

- input and output of data (in, out)
- arithmetic & logic operations (add, subtract, and, or, not)
- instruction sequence changing (branch, jump, compare)
- data transfer (move, load, store).

12. Addressing modes

Instructions may also be grouped according to their **addressing mode**. This is what determines how the operand receives its data. As stated on the previous page the op-code may take the operand from several sources.

13. Main addressing modes

- **Implied addressing** - no operand is required since the op-code instruction is complete in itself, for example, STOP.
- **Direct** or **Absolute addressing** - the address given as the operand is the memory location where the data is stored. For example, SUB M1 means subtract the number stored in address M1 from the number in the accumulator.
- **Immediate addressing** - the operand itself is the data. For example, ADD 5 means add 5 to the number in the accumulator.

Other address modes exist but you do not need to know about them for this course.

Computer Memory

Two types of internal (immediate access) memory exist: **ROM** and **RAM**.

1. Read Only Memory

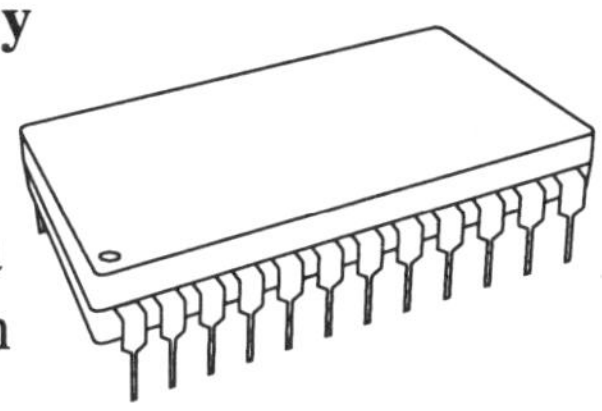

ROM is a permanent storage area for special data and programs which are installed during the process of manufacture. These are 'hard-wired' and cannot be altered by software. Sometimes special ROMs are provided for the user to program. This process requires a special hardware device and is called 'blowing' since each bit is a fusible link which becomes zero when destroyed. Such devices are called PROMS (Programmable ROMS) and the process is irreversible. EPROMS (Erasable PROMS) also exist, where the user can use Ultra Violet light to erase a ROM for reprogramming.

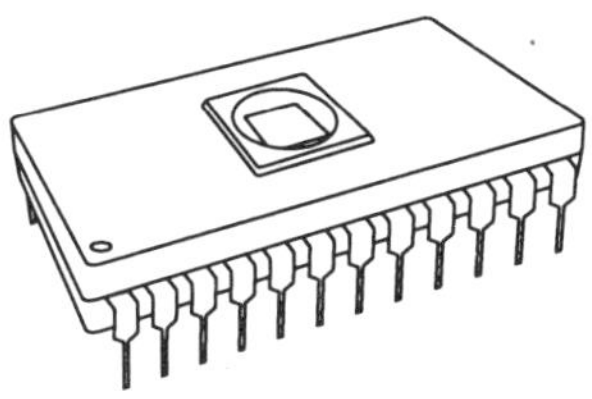

2. Operating systems in ROM

In the older 8-bit micros such as the BBC, the ROM contained all the operating system software but any change or upgrade to the operating system meant changing the ROM chip. Modern micros such as PCs and Macintosh generally have a very simple ROM containing the BIOS (Basic Input/Output System). When powered up, these micros then automatically load the rest of the operating system into RAM from disc. Updates are therefore much simpler since all that is required is a new copy of the system software on a floppy disc.

quick check

Instruction types, addressing modes.
Computer memory - Read Only Memory, operating systems in ROM.

3. Random Access Memory

RAM is the working area of the computer and is used to store programs and data currently being used. Normally when computer memory is quoted in Kb (Kilobytes) it is RAM that is given. The older 8-bit micros had RAM sizes of 32 Kb, 64 Kb and so on. Although these are small by today's standards they were adequate for the software of the 1980s. RAM sizes are now measured in Megabytes (1 Mb = 1024 Kb) since modern WIMP software has high memory requirements. Basic PC and Macintosh systems come supplied with a minimum of 4 Mb of memory. However, sizes of 8 Mb and more are now commonplace, particularly where the user is working in a memory intensive application area such as graphics or sound processing.

4. RAM types

- CMOS RAM - Since RAM is volatile (the contents are lost when power is switched off) many computers now contain a special type of RAM (CMOS) to store setup instructions such as the time, date and colour settings. This memory chip is powered by a battery when the computer is not plugged in and is used because it requires less power than conventional RAM.
- Static RAM (SRAM) - retains its contents as long as power is maintained. It can be written to and read from very quickly but is more expensive to manufacture than DRAM.
- Dynamic RAM (DRAM) - needs to have its contents 'refreshed' (rewritten) every 2 milliseconds. It has slower access than SRAM but more DRAM can be packed onto a single chip.

For economic reasons main memory tends to be made up from DRAM chips which are grouped together on a memory board. For example, 640 Kb of RAM may comprise 2 x 256 Kb and 1 x 128 Kb DRAM chips.

5. Cache memory

A cache memory system tries to provide the higher performance of SRAM but at the lower cost of DRAM. The cache itself is a small amount of very fast access SRAM located between the processor and the main memory. With typical sizes of 16 - 64 Kb its purpose is to hold a copy of frequently used data and code so that the processor can access the faster SRAM, rather than wait for slower DRAM access. Modern processors (e.g. Intel 80486) can incorporate both cache memory and a maths co-processor on one chip. The latest processors (for example, Motorola's 604) have several separate 16 Kb caches allowing true simultaneous operation.

6. Memory maps

Although the computer memory is accessed as one set of continuous locations, it has to be organised in a very efficient way since areas of the memory are used for different purposes. Possible uses include ROM, RAM, cache, graphics and memory mapped I/O. When a computer is built the manufacturer maps out the use to which each block of memory will be put. This may be shown in a special diagram called a memory map. Memory maps are specific to the processors they represent but some similarities exist in all of them.

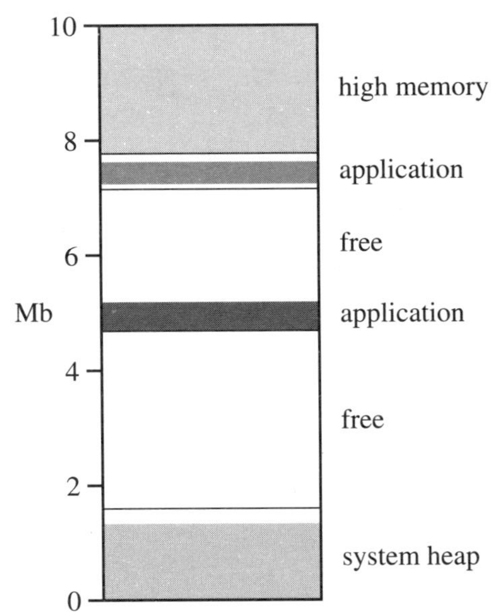

quick check

Random Access Memory, RAM types, cache memory. Memory maps.

Peripherals and Communications

Peripheral Devices

1. Peripherals
Hardware devices external to the CPU and main memory are called **peripherals**. These are used for input, output and backing store and, in effect, connect the CPU with the 'outside world'.

Often the signals produced by the CPU are incompatible with the signals from these peripherals. In this case an interface is required.

2. An interface
is a device, usually hardware, which enables two pieces of equipment which would otherwise be incompatible to communicate with each other. Interfaces vary from simple connections between micro and joystick or micro and printer to full computer systems enabling network communication. Interfaces allow for differences in speed and data between peripherals and the processor.

3. Speed incompatibility
Since modern CPUs work at high speeds, one of the main problems associated with peripherals is speed incompatibility. The CPU, with no moving parts, works very much faster than, say, a CD player or a printer. Several methods are used to try to minimise these problems:

- buffers
- spooling
- peripheral control systems

4. Buffers
To speed up processing, many computers have specialised high speed memory areas called buffers. An input buffer is a waiting area holding blocks of data transferred from a peripheral. An output buffer stores data already processed by the CPU awaiting output (for example, to a printer).

5. Spooling
Simultaneous **P**eripheral **O**peration **On**-**L**ine or **Spooling** is where data is sent to a file on backing store (usually hard disc) until the output device is ready to take it. Spooling takes place as a background process creating temporary files which are automatically removed after use.

6. Peripheral control systems
This is a system which aims to minimise delay and disruption to a processor during data transfer. There are three main approaches to peripheral control:

- polling
- interrupts
- autonomous peripheral operation (DMA).

7. Polling
In a polling system, the processor repeatedly checks the status of each peripheral in turn to see if it has data to be transferred. The checking process is implemented by hardware and is therefore very fast. However, on most occasions there will be no data for transfer so a lot of processor time is used for nothing.

8. Interrupts
In an interrupt system, the CPU does not poll. Instead it continues with its own tasks until an interrupt occurs. It must then stop what it is doing and service the interrupt as quickly as possible, before taking up again where it left off. To enable the processor to do this, it must first preserve the contents of the PC and all the important registers. It does so by placing these (pushing them) into a special area of memory called the stack. On completion of the service the stack contents are 'popped' back to the registers and the processor may then continue with its original task.

quick check

Peripherals and Communications - Peripheral devices. Peripherals. Interface - speed incompatibility. Buffers, spooling. Peripheral control systems - polling, interrupts.

9. Vectored Interrupts

Before servicing an interrupt, the processor must first identify which peripheral caused the interrupt so it can act in an appropriate way. One way of doing this is to use **vectored interrupts**. The interrupting device supplies the processor with a number. This is added to a base number (fixed) to give the address of the memory location containing the jump address (the **vector**) to where the interrupt handling routine lies.

This may seem a cumbersome approach but in reality is a very efficient method of servicing interrupts.

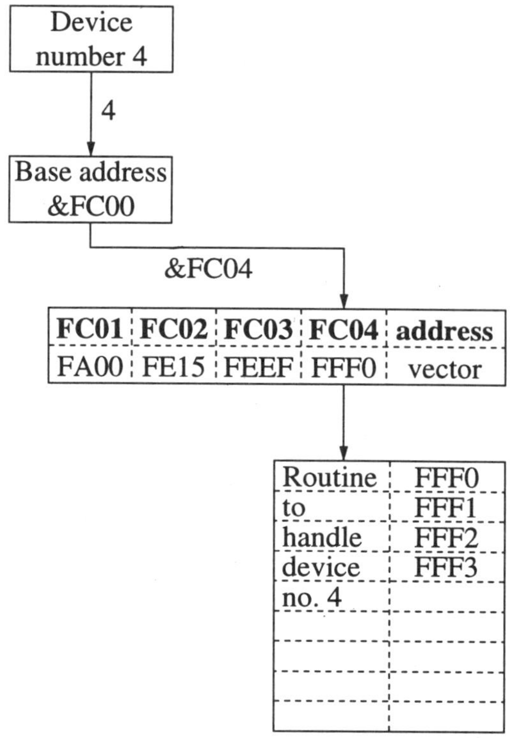

10. Interrupt priorities

Many different devices can cause interrupts, all with different needs in terms of urgency. Some priority system has to be designed to ensure that urgent interrupts are serviced first. Priority ratings are therefore assigned to each interrupt by the operating system. Events such as imminent power failure require servicing immediately and therefore would receive a high priority, whereas events such as printer out of paper would come well down the list. It is possible to 'mask out' some of the lower priority interrupts so that important processing is not interrupted unnecessarily. However, some events (like the power failure) are so important they cannot be masked. These are called **non-maskable interrupts**.

11. Direct memory access (DMA) (autonomous peripheral operation)

One of the slowest processes when handling an interrupt is the saving and restoring of register and PC contents. DMA eliminates the need for temporary storage since it transfers data directly between main memory and the interface of the device in question without using the registers. It replaces the software method by using a special piece of hardware called a **Direct Memory Access Controller (DMAC)**.

Data is transferred as blocks rather than character by character. DMA uses the ability of some devices to act autonomously (after the CPU has given the initial transfer instruction, the device completes the transfer independently). The CPU supplies the DMAC with the start address and the length of the data block. The DMAC 'steals' memory cycles from the CPU which affects its operation only slightly. Most disc drives operate in this way.

quick check

Vectored interrupts. Interrupt priorities. Direct Memory Access.

Transmission of Data

1. Serial and parallel transmission
Devices differ in the way they communicate or 'talk' to each other. One of these differences is in the number of lines (or channels) they use to transmit data.

2. Serial transmission
The binary signals which represent the data are sent one after the other. This requires only one channel. It is more reliable over long distances than other methods.

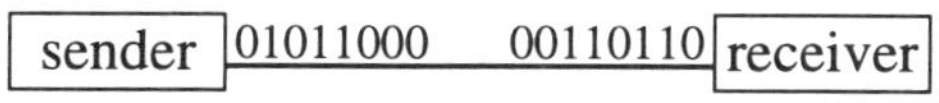

3. Stop and start bits
In practice, more bits than the data itself must be sent during serial transmission. Some method of detecting where data blocks start and stop is required and also some error checking. One common method is to use one start bit and two stop bits to indicate the beginning and end of a data word. A **parity** bit is often added too. This is an extra bit added to make the number of ones in the data up to an odd (odd parity) or even (even parity) number. For example, sending the letter **A** serially:

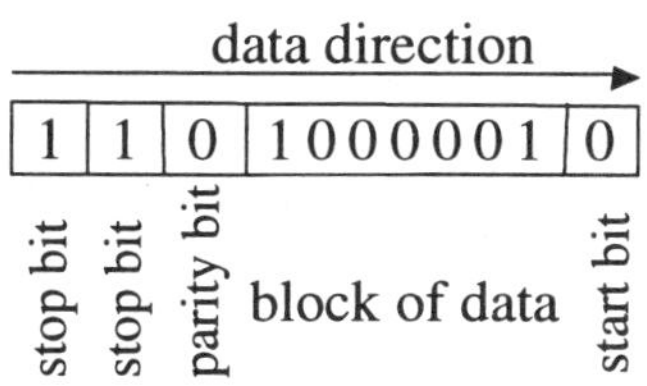

4. Parallel transmission
The data bits are all transmitted as groups. This is much faster than serial transmission but requires more lines. Serial is cheaper and the length of cable is unrestricted. Parallel cable may only transmit a few metres before errors start occurring (skew).

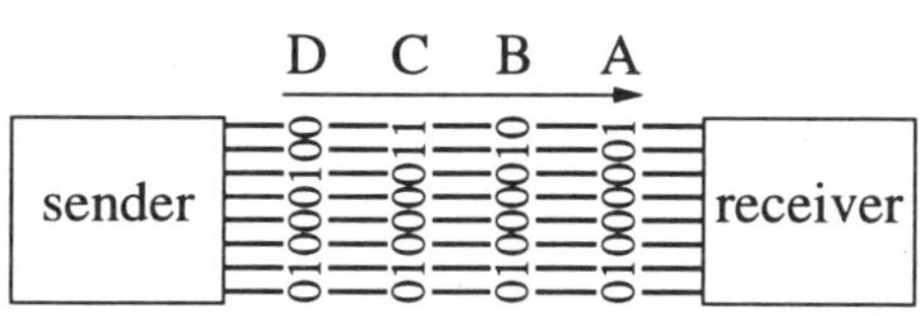

5. Transfer mode
Three modes of data transfer exist:

- **simplex** - data is transferred in one direction only. This may be compared to TV broadcasting where TVs can only receive.
- **half duplex** - data can be transferred in both directions but only one at a time. This may be compared to two-way radios where only one person may speak (and one listen) at any one time.
- **full duplex** - data is transferred in two directions simultaneously. This may be compared to a telephone conversation.

6. Transfer standards
Before two computers can communicate, certain transfer protocols have to be agreed between them. These include **baud rate** (how fast the data is transferred), **data size** (7 or 8 bits), **parity** (odd or even) and **stop bits** (1 or 2). If the two computers do not agree a common format they may try to transmit and receive in totally different ways resulting in corruption or non-receipt of data.

7. Handshaking

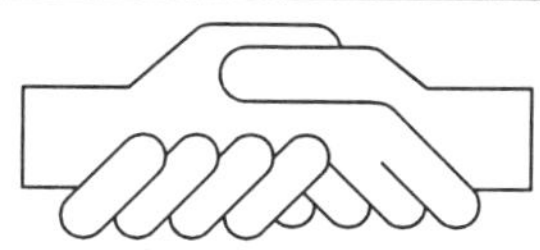

For data transfer to take place successfully, another agreed standard is required. When a peripheral such as a printer is not ready to receive data, and a computer sends data to it, then the data will be corrupted or lost. An elementary conversation therefore takes place between two devices along the lines of this:

> "I have data for you"
> "OK I'm ready for it"
> "Here it comes...."
> "Got it thanks!"

What actually happens electronically is that the computer looks at the printer busy line. If this was not busy, a character would be sent. The printer then acknowledges that the character has arrived and it is ready for the next one. This is called **handshaking**.

quick check

Transmission of data. Serial transmission, stop and start bits. Parallel transmission. Transfer mode, transfer standards. Handshaking.

Backing Store Organisation

Since computer RAM is volatile, backing store is a necessity. Two main classes of backing store exist: **serial access** and **direct** (or **random**) **access**.

1. Magnetic tape - serial access

This remains the least expensive medium for storing large quantities of data. Tapes vary in length from several hundred to a few thousand feet. Modern tapes can store gigabytes of data. The main purpose of tapes now is for backup since they do not have the speed of access of which discs are capable. Although actual data transfer is fast, finding it may take time (it could be at the wrong end of a 3600 feet reel). Data is read in in chunks called **blocks** (between 10 and 10 000 characters) - a block being the amount that fills the buffer. Data transfer is at a set, predetermined speed, therefore the tape must accelerate to this speed, prior to transfer. There are fairly large spaces between blocks of data called **interblock gaps**. These are to allow for the tape to speed up and slow down without any data loss occurring.

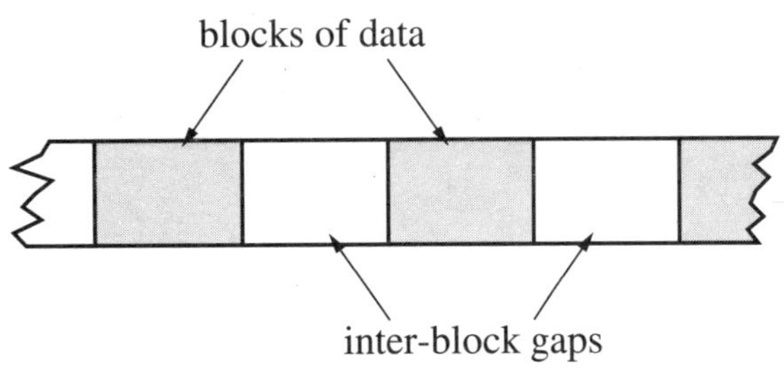

Tape is increasingly being used in the form of a **cartridge** which is easier to use and better protected than the traditional reel-to-reel. Small cartridges are used in **tape streamers**. These are units used as a backup for entire disc contents so that data may be rescued in the event of a disc failure.

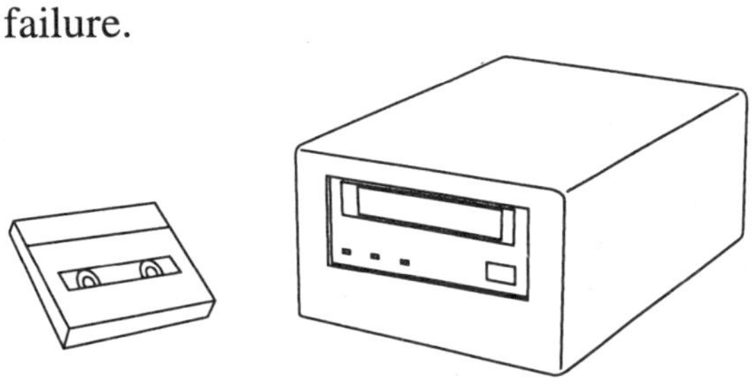

2. Magnetic disc - direct access

Direct access means that data can be read directly from any part of the disc without reading preceding data.

- **Floppy discs** contain a thin plastic disc coated with magnetic material. The outer case supports the disc as it spins round and helps keep dirt off the disc surface. Great care must be taken not to touch the disc surface because it is easily damaged. Typical capacities are between 80 Kb and 1.44 Mb.
- **Hard disc** drives contain one or more rigid discs made from ceramic or aluminium coated with magnetic material. They are sealed into the disc drive unit; this protects them from dirt and careless handling (but they must not be dropped - this can damage them). Hard disc drives are often built into the computer. These typically store from 40 Mb to hundreds of megabytes and even gigabytes.
- **Cylinders** occur in hard disk packs which may contain up to 12 disks. Many read/ write heads move in parallel (in unison) so that any given position aligns the heads with the same track on all discs simultaneously. These are called cylinders (i.e. all the track 5s form cylinder 5).

3. Tracks and sectors

Data on a magnetic disc is stored in a series of concentric tracks which are divided into sectors. The numbers of these can vary but the structure must be written onto the disc when it is formatted or initialised. One layout may be of 80 tracks each divided into 10 sectors.

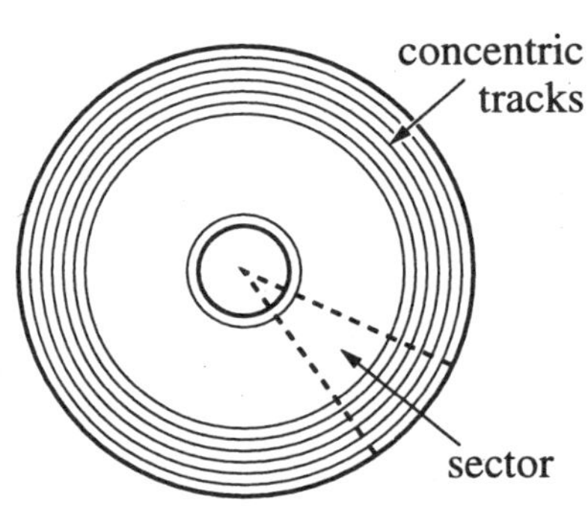

quick check

Backing store organisation. Magnetic tape - serial access. Magnetic disc - direct access. Tracks and sectors.

4. Soft and hard sectoring

There are two different ways of sectoring a disc - **soft** and **hard** sectoring.

- **Soft sectoring** is normally used for floppy discs and involves writing a sector identification number (ID) onto the disc at the beginning of each sector on each track. This occurs during formatting. Since soft sectoring is software determined, it is flexible. This means that the same type of disc can be used with totally different systems, for example, $3\frac{1}{2}$" discs used with both Macintosh and PC computers.

- **Hard sectoring** is usually associated with hard discs. It is permanent and specific to a particular system. It involves marking each sector with a **sector hole** near the spindle. The disk drive then uses a photo-electric cell to detect each hole. The sectors are counted by having an index hole opposite the first sector.

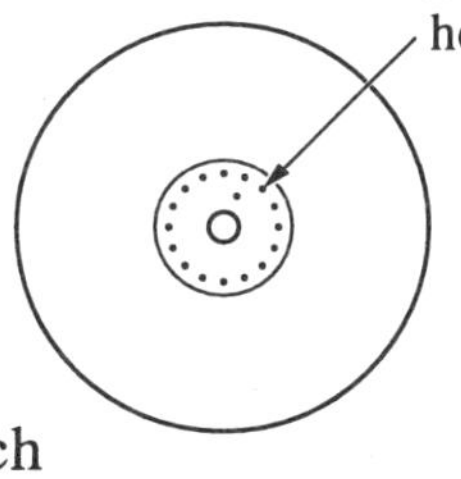

5. Access time

is the time taken for actual data transfer to take place. It varies between 10 and 100 milliseconds for a floppy disc. However, transfer rates between 2.5 Mb and 4 Mb per second are now typical in hard disc systems. The actual access time is defined as:

seek time + search time (latency) + read/write time

- **seek time** is the time taken for the head to move to the required track.
- **search time** is the time taken for the disc to revolve until the data is under the read/ write head (on average, the time for half a revolution of the disc).
- **read/write time** is the time for the actual transfer of data. This is negligible compared to the other two and is often ignored.

6. Other Storage Media

Portability and high storage capacity are important considerations when deciding on what modern storage media to use.

- Writeable CD-ROM devices have fallen in price. A CD-ROM is about 10 cm in diameter and holds about 650 Mb.
It is often used for interactive video and multimedia, where text, pictures, sounds and small film clips are mixed.

- Magneto-optical drives. These combine magnetic media storage with a CD-ROM-like laser read/write head. Faster than CD-ROM but slower than hard drives. Typical capacities are 128, 230 and 384 Mb for the $3\frac{1}{2}$" and 650 Mb and 1.3 Gb for $5\frac{1}{4}$" discs.

- Cartridge Drives are removable hard disc drives which have been on the market for some time but latest products are smaller and lighter (and therefore more portable) than ever before. Two examples are:

  - Iomega Zip drive. This is very lightweight (about 500 g) making it easy to carry around. It contains special floppy cartridges slightly thicker than a standard floppy disc, each of which can hold 100 Mb of storage.

  - SyQuest EZ135 drive. This uses rigid platters rather than floppy media and is therefore faster than Zip. Capacity is 135 Mb per cartridge.

- RAID systems (Redundant Arrays of Independent Discs) make use of the relatively low cost of hard magnetic disc drives. Most of these systems send the data to more than one disc; if data becomes damaged on one then it can be recovered automatically by the system software from another. Damaged drives can be replaced while the system is in use.

quick check

Soft and hard sectoring. Access time.
Other storage media - CD-ROM, magneto-optical, cartridge systems, RAID.

Networks

1. Network
A network is defined as a system (usually computers and associated peripherals) of interconnections of a number of points by various means of communications. The main reason for using a network is the sharing of resources including hardware and information. Two main types of network exist - LAN and WAN.

2. Network topology
describes the various types of network layout. Many names exist for layouts but there are four main categories:

- **Centralized network** - all communications pass through a central node (or connection). A node can be a simple multiplexer or a dedicated computer system.
  - **star topology**

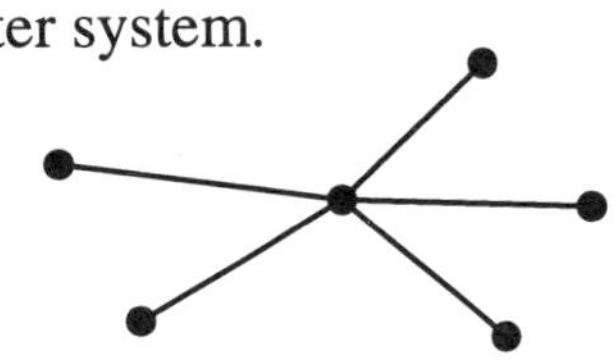

  A typical use for this type of network would be many users connected to a centralized database.
- **Distributed network** - fully (or partially) connected with all nodes connecting to all other nodes. A typical example of this would be ARPANET in the U.S.
  - **mesh topology**

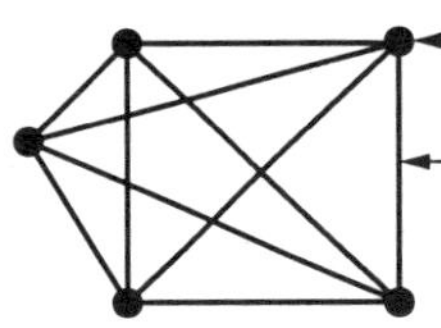

- **Ring network** - also known as a loop. Messages are passed around the chain. If a message is not destined for a particular station, it is boosted then passed onto the next. An example is the Cambridge ring.

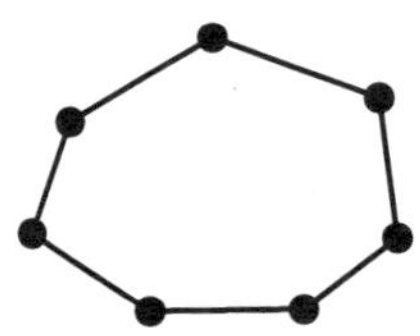

- **Bus network** - so called because of its similarity to the bus architecture inside a computer. A single node may fail without upsetting the rest. A typical example is ETHERNET. Most school networks are based on bus topology.

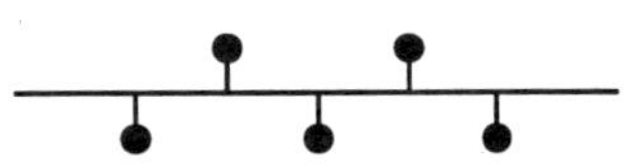

3. Local area network (LANs)
A network linking several computers and peripherals in the same local area (room, building, site). Linked by cable up to distances of several kilometres.

- Benefits include:
  - Sharing of hardware (e.g. printers, discs)
  - Sharing of information (may be centrally stored)
  - Communications between users.
- Characteristics:
  - Low error rate (one bit in several million)
  - Usually ring or bus topology
  - Fast transfer rates (e.g. 1 - 20 Mbit/s)
  - Usually same sort of equipment used.
- Advantages:
  - Resources shared - cuts down on numbers of printers and other peripherals required
  - Files shared - updating done centrally and only once - all users have access to update
  - Easy to add new systems as and when required.
- Disadvantages:
  - Security/privacy - it is not always desirable to share all the data on a network with all the users. Security systems such as different levels of passwords are used here to give different levels of access.
  - Security is also concerned with prevention of data loss therefore provision for regular backup of files must also be made.
  - Incompatibility - different file formats may cause communication problems. For example, two different computers on the same network may use different standards, or different manufacturers for the same machine may use different file formats. To a great extent this problem has disappeared in recent years with the advent of translators for changing one file format into another.

quick check

Networks. Network topology - centralised, distributed, ring, bus.
Local Area Networks benefits, characteristics, advantages, disadvantages.

4. **CSMA/CD - Carrier Sense Multiple Access/Collision Detection**
   prevents data collisions from two or more stations broadcasting simultaneously.
   - Carrier sense - before sending (talking) stations listen to see if a carrier signal is already present. If so they wait.
   - Multiple access - stations broadcast any time they sense the channel is free.
   - Collision detection - if two stations wish to transmit at the same time, both will sense that the channel is free and therefore may collide. The collision detection mechanism causes both devices to stop, listen and try again after a random time interval. Each device must wait a different time (only millionths of a second). If after several retries they still collide, an error message is generated.

5. **LAN hardware requirements**
   Typical hardware requirements for a modern LAN are:

   - **Workstation** - a microcomputer in its own right with local processing capability but also access to shared resources.

   - **Servers** - these allocate shared resources to other network nodes. A number of different types exist, categorized according to the resources they control.
     - File server - usually a microcomputer based on a powerful processor such as 68000 series or intel 80486 (more recently could be PowerPC600 series or Pentium processors). Handles access to all shared storage, files and directories. Some file servers can control several different disks.
     - Communications server - needed when a LAN requires access to an external network or database. Links usually established through bridges or gateways.
     - Print server - accepts jobs from any workstation and automatically spools these into a print queue. It may also assign priorities to important jobs whatever their position in the queue.

6. **Wide area networks (WANs)**
   A WAN is a network of computers on a much larger scale than a LAN. It may contain one or more LANs within itself. WANs differ from LANs in that the computers used are usually much further apart. Data transfer between WAN stations tends to be slow compared to LANs (typical speeds range from 300 Kbits/s to 1.54 Mbits/s). It is also more error prone. This is because WANs are routed through the telephone network and therefore may suffer interference. They use different types of cable and may even use satellites.
   - **Packet Switching** (**PS**) - many WANs make use of the PS service which allows data transfer at a lower cost than phone lines. A local phone call is used to access the PS network which then takes over the routing. PS operates by breaking data into **data packets** which are then sent throughout the WAN under computer control. Switching computers are located at each node on the network and these control and monitor each data packet. As well as the data itself packets must contain other information such as the source identifier, the destination address, the sequence of the packet in the completed message and the detection and control of transmission errors.
   - The current most popular WAN is the **Internet** - a series of computers owned by commercial companies, universities etc., which has gradually grown to be enormous. Many people, who had never used computers previously, now use the Net as a matter of course for E-mail (electronic mail), other forms of communication and for access to the huge amount of data it makes accessible.
   - **Information providers** - for a small fee provide access to Internet for small users. Demon, Compuserve, Cityscape and eWorld are typical providers.
   - Other WANs include ARPANET, PDN, DATAPAC and JANET but these can now all be accessed via the Internet and the World Wide Web (WWW).

quick check

CSMA/CD. LAN hardware requirements.
Wide Area Networks - packet switching, Internet, information providers.

Transmission Media and Errors

When data is to be transferred between computers or peripherals, one of the important considerations is the media to be used. The type of media chosen determines the transfer rate between the devices.

1. Twisted wire pair

The simplest method to communicate between two devices is in a **twisted wire** pair. This consists of two conductors (wires) separated from each other by insulation in a cable. Bit rates are relatively slow (1 Mbps over distances up to 100 m) and even slower for longer distances. However, the cable is cheap and easy to install.

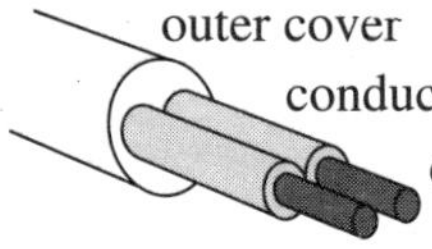

2. Coaxial cable

For faster bit rates **coaxial cable** is more appropriate. Since the current tends to flow along the outer skin of a conductor, a different design of cabling is necessary. In coaxial cable one conductor is 'surrounded' by the other with a layer of insulation between. This allows for faster transfer (up to 20 Mbps) and has been in use for a long time as TV/video cable.

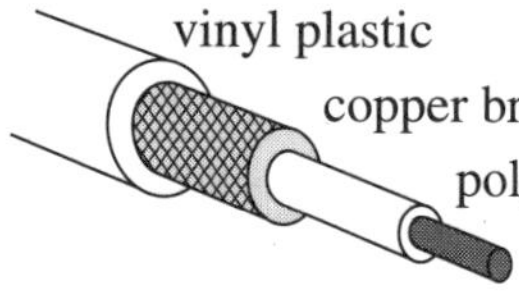

3. Fibre optic cable

However good the quality of cable, there eventually becomes a point where electrical transmission reaches its limits. Interference from other signals, poor insulation and other random fluctuations mean that traditional methods are limited. Instead, **light** can be used to transfer signals. **Fibre optic** cables are made from glass. LEDs or lasers are used to transmit light along them. The bit rate is much faster (140 Mbit/s) but the disadvantage is cost. However, many major communications companies are making increasing use of this technology.

4. Microwaves

All the above methods have the limitation of a physical medium to carry the signal. Instead, data may be transferred through the air (and indeed space), by use of electromagnetic radio waves (microwaves). These can carry large volumes of data at high rates over long distances. However, the costs are high and lack of security can be a problem. Despite this, increasingly large numbers of satellites are in use in this way.

5. Errors

It is almost impossible to transmit data without some errors occurring. This is usually due to interference on the lines. Various methods of reducing these errors are now employed.

- Causes of errors
  - noise - extra signals from a variety of sources can corrupt data.
  - distortion - existing signals are altered, often by skewing (the bits becoming misaligned) during parallel transmission.
  - miscellaneous - e.g. faulty components.
- Detecting errors
  - One of the simplest and most common methods of error detection is the use of a **parity** bit (see page 39). This will only highlight simple errors and if more than one bit is affected then parity checks will not detect it.
  - A better method is use of a **checksum**. This involves adding blocks of data together numerically and taking part of the answer (often the 16 least significant bits) as an extra number (the checksum) which is added to the end of the block of data. When the data is received the same calculation is performed and the two checksum values are compared.

quick check

Transmission media - twisted wire pair, coaxial cable, fibre optic cable, microwaves.
Errors - causes, detection.

Operating Systems

1. Software

There are two categories of software - **applications** and **systems**. Applications software performs the actual tasks the user wants, such as word-processing, stock control or games. Systems software controls the inner working of the machine. It consists of programs such as compilers, interpreters, assemblers and utilities but the major part is the **operating system**.

2. The operating system

acts as a buffer between the user and the inner workings of the computer. It controls all the complex tasks essential to everyday running of any computer system and manages all the resources of that system, such as the CPU, file handling, backing store, I/O and memory.

3. Operating system structure

Any OS can be viewed as a series of levels. At the lowest end of the system is the core which remains in memory permanently when the computer is running. This is called the **executive** or **kernel**. Its main purpose is to carry out process scheduling and interrupts. In modern computers, the remainder of the OS is normally held on a direct access medium (such as hard or floppy disc) where parts may be read in as required.

- Input/Output system (I/O)
  controls the data flow between main memory and peripherals connected to the CPU. It enables the user to treat all peripheral devices as if they had the same characteristics (which they do not!).
- Memory management
  allocates main memory to programs and data as and when they require it, since main memory is too small to hold them all at any one time.
- File handling
  allows the user to treat the many different types of files that exist in the same way. It facilitates access to all file types and ensures that only one program can retrieve a particular record from a file, at one time.

3. Operating system structure (cont.)

- Command Language Interpreter
  is the top level of the OS and allows communication between it and the user. This may be directly with the OS (for example, * commands on a BBC system) or through applications. Modern computer systems have a graphical user interface (GUI) which communicates with the OS through a mouse and the use of icons. In this case the user is 'protected' from the OS itself since all its operations go on 'behind the scenes'.

4. Kernel

In single user, single process systems (which includes most microcomputers) the only process is the user program. The purpose of the kernel is to allocate the CPU to this program but also to any other processes created by it. These may include: disc read/write, printing and A to D conversions. The kernel also maintains the current status of any process during the servicing of an **interrupt**. In **multi-tasking** systems the kernel must also:

- hold descriptions for more than 1 process
- communicate between processes
- initiate several processes simultaneously.

5. The Input/Output system

links peripherals and the CPU. It allows the user to treat output to a variety of devices, such as printers, screen, disc drives and plotters in the same way. All output is treated as **files** using the file management system and the job of the I/O is to translate these various output signals into commands specific to the peripheral for which they are intended. The user does not need to know what is going on or to worry about different transfer rates, data formats or communication methods.

quick check

Software, operating system. Structure of operating system.
Kernel, Input/output system.

6. Memory management

In a single process system (such as MS-DOS, Acorn MOS or CP/M) the memory management facilities are not particularly sophisticated, since only one application is resident at one time. The memory is divided into two areas: one for the OS and the other (sometimes called the **Transient Process Area** or **TPA**) for the user programs. The task of the memory management program is to make sure the user program will fit into the TPA and protect the OS from being overwritten.

In some systems (such as the BBC) the OS is entirely in ROM making it simple to protect since it cannot be overwritten. Updating such an OS is difficult, however, since it means replacing a chip. In more modern systems only a small part of the OS is on ROM. This is known as the **bootstrap loader** and its purpose is to load in the rest of the OS from disc.

7. Memory protection

If large parts of the OS are placed in RAM they are vulnerable to user programs which may overwrite them. It is therefore essential that some protection exists so that the OS does not become corrupted. There are two common protection methods:

- **Fence registers** contain an address pointing to the last byte of the OS. Any address to which a program tries to write is checked against this and if it is 'over the fence' (the wrong side), the write operation will not take place.

- **Protection bits** - one bit of each memory location in RAM is used as a protection bit. If the bit is set high (to 1) the user may not use it; if it is 0 then the write operation may proceed. Some system programs have privileged access since they may need to write to this protected area under special circumstances.

8. Directories

All files held on backing store are kept track of by means of **directories**. This is a list of all known file names. Two types of directory structure exist:

- **single level** - one directory contains information about all the files on a given disc. This is a simple structure but is inflexible. Often too many files exist at one level. File names may accidentally be repeated overwriting the original file and protection of some files, but not others, is difficult.
- **hierarchical** - This is a more structured system where directories may contain other directories which may also contain directories, and so on, in a tree structure. It is normal to group similar files within one directory with the one at the top of the hierarchy being the 'root'. This method allows for simpler protection of chosen files by simply grouping them in a directory with restricted access.

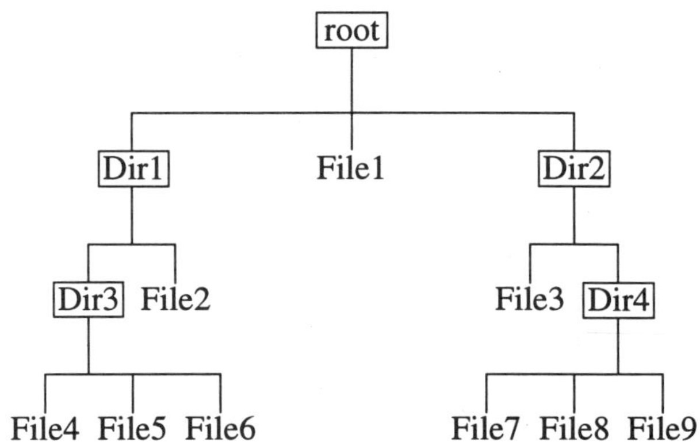

Directories can hold other directories or files with the same or different access privileges. Dir4 above could be private, locking files 7, 8 & 9 to all but high level users. File access may be **read**, **write**, or **execute** at any level. Also, access rights may be different for different groups of users such as the owner, the owner's group or guests (all others). In reality often the owner will have full access but guests may be given execute-only or read-only access.

quick check

Memory management, memory protection. Directories - single level, hierarchical.

9. Pathnames

A pathname is the full specification of a file-name - its full title reading from the root directory. In the previous example, the full pathname for file9 would be:

Root.Dir2.Dir4.File9

This can lead to long file names so users may select a CSD (Current Selected Directory) which all files will be written to or read from until further notice, or unless full pathnames are given.

10. Logical and physical files

The directories described above are the user's view of file storage. These are called

- **Symbolic file directories** (**SFDs**). It is important to realise that the actual files themselves are not stored in this way. This is simply a convenience for the user.
- **A Basic file directory** (**BFD**) exists and it contains information about how the files are actually stored. This includes the file:
    - ID code - identification number 1,2,3...
    - type - e.g. TXT, DIR, BAT
    - size - length in number of bytes
    - access attributes - Read, Write, Exec
    - physical address (where it actually starts on disc).

  Note that the user name is not included (this is in the SFD). The BFD is itself a file and it too must be stored somewhere.

11. Disc management

handles the allocation of disc space, including which blocks are allocated (in use). It must keep track of blocks freed when files are deleted and how many blocks are available for new files. Files occupy whole blocks, even if part of a block is not required. Partially filled blocks at the end of files are wasted space since the next file to be written will start with a new block.

When a disc is initialised (or formatted) some space is allocated to the directory structure and so is unavailable for storing files.

12. Allocation of disc space

Two main methods are used to allocate files disc space: **contiguous** and **non-contiguous**.

13. Contiguous allocation

involves writing files to blocks which are physically adjacent. A file starts on one block and continues to occupy consecutive blocks until it is stored.

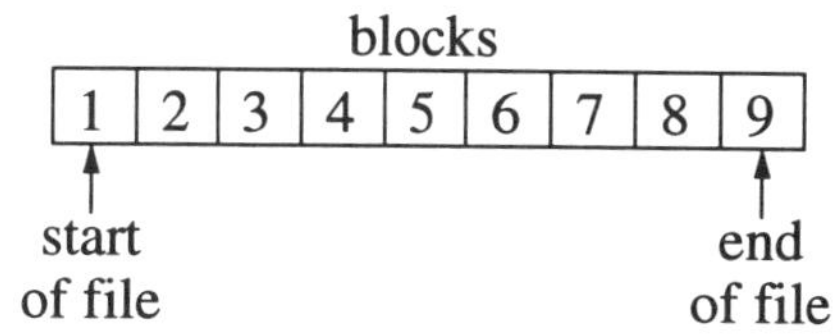

- Advantages of this method are: speed, little space needed to store details.
- Disadvantages are that as files are added and deleted, areas of space are wasted since files are different lengths and one will not completely fill the space left by another (disc fragmentation). Disc compacting (shuffling all files up to put space at the end) will cure this.

14. Fitting files into free space

After being used for some time, a disc will have spaces of different sizes scattered throughout its storage space. These are where files have been stored and then deleted. A method of determining which space to allocate to any new files, must be determined. Two common methods are:

- **First fit** - any new file is allocated to the first space big enough to hold it. The area may be just bigger than the file or very much bigger. The advantage of this method is that little searching needs to be done to find a space; the disadvantage is that a large amount of space may be wasted with disc fragmentation becoming a problem.
- **Best fit** - all the free space is examined and the one which is closest in size (but bigger) than the file being written, is used to store it. The advantage of this is that it greatly reduces internal fragmentation. A longer search time is required, however.

quick check

Pathnames. Logical and physical files. Disc management.
Allocation of disc space - contiguous allocation, fitting files into free space.

15. Non-contiguous allocation

Using this method, files are written to disc using blocks which do not have to be physically adjacent. They must be linked in some way so the file can be retrieved and this may be done in two ways: **chaining** and **indexing**.

16. Chaining

Each physical block of the file contains a pointer to the next block. It is important to distinguish between **logical** and **physical** blocks. The logical blocks of a file are numbered to show the sequence of the actual file contents (1,2,3,4,5....). The physical blocks are numbered according to where the file is stored on the disc and the order may be very disordered, for example 14,11,13,16

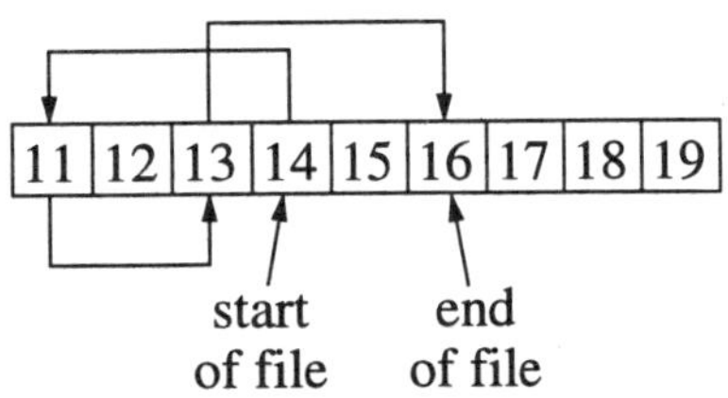

The storage information for the file looks like this:	Logical block	Physical block
	1	14
	2	11
	3	13
	4	16

17. Indexing

The second method of implementing non-contiguous allocation of files is by indexing. This is similar to chaining in that pointers link the file blocks together, but this time the pointers are stored in a separate block called the **index block**. Each file on the disc has its own index block containing pointers to all the blocks used in storing that particular file. Using the same example as above, the file storage now looks like this:

11	12	13	14	15	16	17	18	19

1	14
2	11
3	13
4	16

contents of index block

18. Indexing v. chaining

- Chaining - advantages
  - fast - since each block accessed contains the address of the next one required.
  - The address of the first file block is all that is needed in the BFD.
  - free blocks easily chained together.
  - no fragmentation since all free blocks are useable.
- Chaining - disadvantages
  - slow - since access to each block can only come through the previous one.
  - if chain is broken, the file is lost beyond the broken pointer.

- Indexing - advantages
  - no fragmentation.
  - faster for random access operation since only the index block and the files required need to be accessed; there is no need to follow the chain through all the preceding blocks first.
- Indexing - disadvantages
  - index blocks may take a lot of space.

19. Command language interpretation

One of the most important functions of the OS is to interpret the command language which allows the user to communicate with it. Generally, two types of language are recognised:

- command language
- job control language

20. Command language

A command language interpreter (CLI) accepts command lines, checks them for syntax and then passes on the relevant requests to the OS. Typical commands could be:

- display directory contents (catalog)
- delete files from disc
- copy files from one disc to another
- change access rights to files
- verify discs

Simple commands may be typed in at the keyboard (like *catalog on BBC) but more complex operations may be stored in command or batch files (as in MS-DOS).

quick check

Non-contiguous allocation - chaining, indexing.
Command language interpretation, command language.

21. Job control language

is associated with batch processing operating systems. JCLs allow details of job requirements to be specified to the OS For example:

```
BEGIN
    JOB 9846
    COMPILE pay.cob (disk 3)
    LOAD pay.obj (disk 3)
    RUN
END
```

This series of commands identifies the job, compiles a COBOL program, loads the resultant object program and then runs it.

22. Graphical user interface (GUI)

Modern computer systems make use of a WIMP-type GUI. All operating system utilities are selected via a mouse or tracker ball, from icons on the screen. The GUI then communicates these commands to the CLI which interprets them and passes them on to the OS in the normal way. A GUI is another level of interface between the user and the CLI but its great advantage is that inexperienced computer users have access to otherwise complex OS commands.
For example, compare clicking and dragging a file from floppy to hard disc on a Macintosh (file copying) to its equivalent in MS-DOS:

```
COPY A:\filename.BAT  C:\newfile.BAT
```

23. Subroutines

The operating system is a complex collection of programs which perform the tasks necessary to operate the computer. Although these can all be accessed at OS level (via MS-DOS commands or by point and click with a mouse) they are also required by the application programs and higher level languages which run within the computer. For example, in program management the following are possible:

- loading a program
- saving a program
- running a program

23. Subroutines (cont.)

Within higher level programming languages such as BASIC or Pascal, it is possible to make use of more complex OS routines.
For example, file handling programs must be able to:

- create random and sequential files
- open these for reading and writing
- read and write records/bytes to files
- close files.

24. Multi-tasking

A modern OS is able to cope with more than one process at any one time. This is because peripherals are slow compared to the processor and therefore it is often idle while waiting for various peripherals to catch up. Multi-tasking is a technique which makes use of this idle time to allocate other jobs to the processor.
Several programs reside in the TPA at one time and the processor shares its time between them. This **apparent concurrency** is possible since any one job will have 'idle time' allowing others use of the processor. In an ideal situation one of the user programs will be more processor intensive than the other. For example, during word-processing it is common to have a print-job on-going in the background. The word-processing is interactive but the printing is not, therefore the printing is a background task.

25. Memory mapping

In a multitasking situation, the **kernel** has a far greater role to play than in a single process operation, particularly in terms of memory management, processor scheduling and peripheral sharing. If two or more programs are in the TPA at one time, it is crucial that they do not occupy the same area of memory since one would overwrite the other. It is also important that the process can function anywhere in the TPA (not specific to any particular addresses).
This involves **memory mapping** which is commonly done by:

- bank switching
- base limit addressing.

quick check

Job control language, graphical user interface.
Subroutines, Multi-tasking. Memory mapping.

26. Bank switching

Several programs exist in memory at one time, each with identical address space. A **bank selection register** is used to select between physical banks. This is the basis of the BBC sideways RAM memory, although this is not multitasking since only one RAM may be active at any one time. It is based on the **terminate and stay resident** principle where several programs are present but only one is actually in use (active) at any one time.

For example, the BBC Master contains several ROM chips including BASIC, VIEW and VIEWSHEET. Since these are in ROM, they are all present each time the BBC is switched on. However, since they all occupy the same memory (from address &8000) only one may be selected at any time. A command such as *SHEET issued after switching on, would enable the spreadsheet program but disable BASIC.

27. Base limit addressing

is more flexible since it allows the memory to be divided into different size segments, thus allowing different length programs to utilise it. As each program is loaded in, a **process descriptor** is created. This holds the address at which the program has loaded (the **base address**) and also the program length (**the limit address**). When the next program loads, it starts from the next free byte after the limit.

28. Scheduling

One function of the OS is to determine which programs in the memory should be next allocated processor time. Several criteria must be satisfied when deciding allocation of processor time, for example:

- the maximum number of jobs should be processed in the minimum time.
- no peripheral should be underused.
- interactive users must be allocated a fair share (or they may think the system has 'hung').
- no job should be repeatedly sent to the back.

28. Scheduling (cont.)

A part of the kernel called the **dispatcher** or **low level scheduler** allocates the actual processes to the CPU. Note that a process is not a program but a series of actions produced by the execution of some program instructions. The dispatcher must record the current status of each process from the following possibilities:

- it is **running** (it has the processor)
- it is **free** (it would run if it had the processor)
- it is **blocked** (the process is suspended or unable to run because it is waiting for input or output).

A **process descriptor table** records the status of each program and the dispatcher refers to it before deciding how to allocate the processor time. It does this each time there is an interrupt.

29. Time sharing

refers to allocation of CPU **time slices** to a number of user programs in a multiprogramming environment. A time share OS is intended to keep users busy, as opposed to a batch multiprogramming system which keeps the processor busy. Time slices are controlled by a real time clock which generates very regular, frequent pulses; each slice is very short (about 100 milliseconds). Slices are allocated either by:

- **Priority scheduling** where jobs are given a priority rating or by
- **Round Robin scheduling** where each is offered an equal slice in turn.

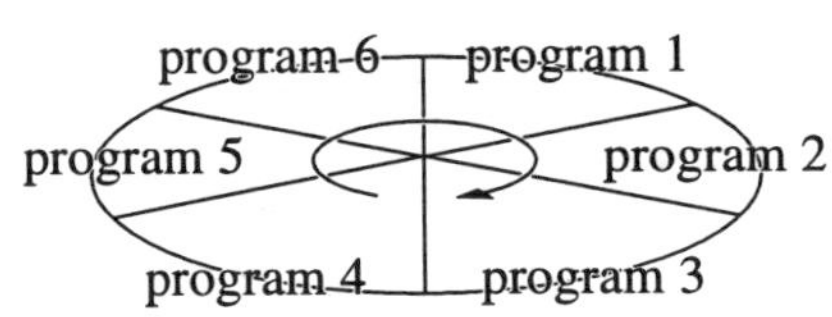

quick check

Bank switching, base limit addressing. Scheduling. Time sharing.

30. Processing types

A variety of different processing environments exist, classified according to the ways in which they control data. Two of the most important of these are:

- batch processing
- on-line processing.

31. Batch processing

A batch processing system is one which processes groups or 'batches' of data at regular intervals. The data tends to be large volume and identical in form, for example payroll. Usually when a batch process is running, there is no requirement for user interaction. It is often the case that data can be encoded **off-line** - not under the direct control of the processor.

- Disadvantages
  Batch is normally a slow turnaround process and often there may be a delay of hours or even days between collecting transactions and receiving the processed results.
- Advantages
  Batch processing gives many opportunities for controlling data accuracy since timing is not critical. It is commonly used, therefore, when immediate update of files is not required.

32. On-line processing

If a peripheral such as a VDU or keyboard is on-line, it is under the direct control of the CPU. The advantage of such processing is that the turnaround between data collection and data processing is greatly reduced. There are two main methods of on-line processing:

- **real time processing** - was initially developed to control process systems where, for example, the constituents of a chemical process have to be kept at set proportions. Any fluctuation in this must immediately be remedied by linking a computer system to control valves. Real time processing has now developed further because of improvements in microprocessors. It now features in many diverse areas such as car engine management systems and automated production lines (in CNC machines). The important feature of all of these is that the speed of the processor to react to a change in circumstances is crucial.
- **time share processing** - occurs when the CPU allocates time slices to several users in a multi-user operating system as described earlier (see page 50, section 29).

33. Operating system levels

The user's view of the operating system is like the Russian dolls - all that can be seen is the outer layer.

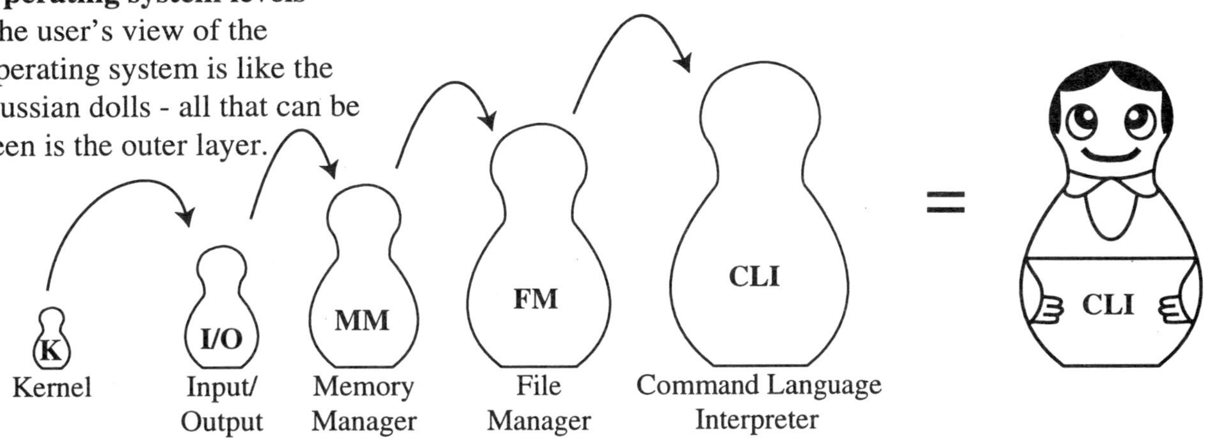

processes, flags	data blocks	segments, pages	files, devices	environment, data	**objects**
create, destroy, resume, suspend, signal, wait	read, write, allocate, free	read, write, fetch	create, destroy, open, close, read, write	command language statement	**operations**

quick check

Processing types - batch processing, on-line processing. Operating System levels.

Developments in Computing

Computing has developed at an incredible rate since its infancy in the early 1940s. Progress has meant that we now have more power and speed at lower cost and in smaller machines than ever before. One catalyst to this change has been the Second World War, which led to the initial interest in, and need for, computing. Another was the Space Race, the desire to reach the moon in the 1960s.

1. Developments in architecture

Several major inventions have led to separate periods of computer development - these are known as generations of computers:

- first generation - 1940s & 1950s use of electronic valves
- second generation - Late 1950s & 1960s invention of the transistor and the use of PCBs made computers smaller, more economical and reliable.
- third generation - Late 1960s & early 1970s saw several transistors and other components being joined onto a single base. These were known as integrated circuits or silicon chips. This was called small scale integration (SSI) and medium scale integration (MSI).
- fourth generation - from the late 1970s until the present day, first large (LSI) and now very large (VLSI) scale integration means many components on a single chip.
- fifth generation - modern techniques such as using transputers for parallel processing (many processors working together - in parallel - to speed up the effectiveness of the CPU) and multiprocessing (where several separate programs may run simultaneously but each having control of only one processor) have led to higher speeds. The structure of computer language has also changed with current emphasis on declarative languages such as prolog, parlog and occam.
- sixth generation - if processing power continues to improve at current rates, developments such as voice recognition and AI use in expert systems will bring the dawn of a new computer age with powerful processing power accessible and affordable to all.

2. Measuring computer performance

One of the biggest challenges in modern computer development has been finding ways to increase processing speed. Various conventions are used to quote computer speeds or throughput, including MIPS (millions of instructions per second) and MOPS (millions of operands per second). However, both of these ignore word length, therefore memory bandwidth (millions of bits per second) is regarded as a better measure.

3. Increasing computer throughput

Processing speed can be increased using:

- increased clock speed
- increased bus width
- interleaving
- lookahead processors
- pipeline processors.

4. RISC architecture

It is generally recognised that the greatest increases in processor speed can be obtained by changes in the system architecture. One of the most significant of these is in use of **R**educed **I**nstruction **S**et **C**omputers. This is a relatively new concept where only a small number of instructions (compared to the processor norm) are used. However, since these instructions are deliberately simple, the processor can operate at many times the speed of processors with more complex instruction sets. RISC machines are effective because the average processor spends most of its time on simple instructions such as ADD, SUB, LOAD, STORE and BRANCH. Other features are many internal registers, fewer register-to-memory transfers and wide data paths.

quick check

Developments in architecture. Measuring computer performance. Increasing computer throughput. RISC architecture.

Printed by Inglis Allen, Kirkcaldy